Visual Thinking Strategies

*Using Art to Deepen Learning
Across School Disciplines*

Philip Yenawine

HARVARD EDUCATION PRESS
CAMBRIDGE, MASSACHUSETTS

Library of Congress Control Number 2013941189
Paperback ISBN 978-1-61250-609-8
Library Edition ISBN 978-1-61250-610-4

Published by Harvard Education Press,
an imprint of the Harvard Education Publishing Group

Harvard Education Press
8 Story Street
Cambridge, MA 02138

Cover Design: Steven Pisano
Cover Photo: Fuse/Getty Images

The typefaces used in this book are Berkeley Old Style, and ITC Legacy Sans.

Visual Thinking Strategies

CONTENTS

PREFACE

WE WHO CARE ABOUT KIDS and what they learn have been given an interesting challenge recently. The learning sought by the Common Core Standards Initiative raises the bar a great deal from existing standards and the testing designed to assess achievement. An expanded set of skills is moving to center stage in the classroom. Students will need to demonstrate their abilities to think critically, problem-solve effectively, reason clearly, listen constructively, and speak and write persuasively. Students will need to show they understand what they are learning; not just memorizing but comprehending the problems to be solved; not just solving but knowing how they did it and how to do it again; not just assimilating information and ideas but putting them into operation in and out of class; not just performing assignments but learning how to learn.

How will they achieve this growth, long considered elusive?

Part of the answer, I believe, can be found in the book you are now holding.

This book will explain a fairly simple addition to classroom practice called Visual Thinking Strategies (VTS) that can extend teacher capacity and student performance. With VTS, teachers deeply embed art into the classroom experience and then build on that base, achieved in very little time, to apply the carefully calibrated yet simple questions to other lessons where students freely engage and develop both individually and as a group. Simply and briefly, teachers using the VTS protocol can increase class participation and student engagement while deepening the thinking, language ability, writing skills, and visual literacy of all their students in as few as ten hour-long discussions a year. VTS equips students to meet Common Core standards in a simple, doable, real, and substantial way.

How do I know?

VTS got its start at New York City's Museum of Modern Art in 1991 in response to a challenge from our Board of Trustees, who wanted to be certain visitors were learning from our education programs. As education director at MOMA from 1983 to 1993, I responded to the challenge and worked with my colleagues to develop VTS with the intent to build visual literacy. We turned to teachers to help us see if we could achieve growth in viewing skills with sets of lessons, and during twelve years of field research, we determined that VTS achieved its objectives but did a lot more besides.

In 1995, we formed the nonprofit Visual Understanding in Education (VUE) to fund and execute the research as well as to train teachers to use VTS, eventually developing a K–6 curriculum with offshoots (not discussed in the book) for middle and high school.[1] Over time, we have worked with more than four thousand teachers who have implemented the image lessons of VTS; many of them have also applied the VTS facilitation method to explore math, science, social studies, and other subjects.

For students, VTS builds a variety of related skills: visual literacy, complex thinking and the language to express it, listening, increasing interest in and capacity to write, and collaborative problem solving. For teachers, it provides a strategy to bring out students who often hang back, to level the field, to introduce discussion as a vehicle for collective meaning making that extends across disciplines, and to establish a clear means of scaffolding students' abilities/peer learning.

Even before the adoption of the Common Core standards, I wanted to write a book for teachers who seek to engage more students more often in the intriguing process of their own learning. I've wanted to argue that effective teaching involves a good deal more than achieving proficiency on standardized tests. I've wanted to share a practical application of constructivism, one that allows students to stretch their senses of themselves and their capabilities, one that I truly believe helps them become their best selves. I've wanted to share the fruits of more than twenty years of work leading to a method teachers can easily learn to reach all students: helping those who struggle to succeed, encouraging those for whom learning is easy to work to their potential, and striving for all to go beyond the fairly low denominators of "proficiency." That VTS also provides ways to meet many of the day-to-day Common Core standards and, importantly, to achieve the overarching goals of making students college- and employment-ready, is icing on the cake.

This book responds to requests from hundreds of teachers, principals, and others who are looking for a new paradigm that nurtures deeper learning as a counterpoint to repetitive exercises and standardized tests. Most want reinforcement as they address existing priorities—elusive in too many circumstances—regarding language, math, and other subjects, but they want to go beyond them as well.

Although VTS has been available through VUE since 2000, there has been no document relating its history and, importantly, its application by teachers. This book tells the story of how and why it was developed and how it has been applied by some of the many hundreds of elementary school teachers—"normal," hardworking, competent professionals—who have put VTS to use in their classrooms. Its purpose is to present and explain their experience. I illustrate VTS with examples and present its basis in research, its impact on thinking and language skills, its application by teachers to help their students explore many subjects, its function in meeting and exceeding certain standards, its influence on school cultures, and its potential for making all teachers "effective."

This book also illustrates how VTS appears in classrooms of differing age and grade levels and how different teachers with specific populations—English language learners, for example, or special needs students—apply it to achieve desired outcomes. I provide samples of work by students, all identified by pseudonyms.

If I am successful, you will want to know more. At the end of the book, I include an appendix giving practical information to those who want to try VTS in their schools or classrooms. There are also additional links to research and professional development opportunities available through VUE, considered useful for most who implement VTS.

Using VTS, teachers have seen marked impact on students as early as preschool. They have turned developmental and environmentally acquired differences in readiness among students into an advantage. They've seen older students recharged even after feeling the sting of failure. They've seen significant achievement in students who struggle. They've seen students for whom learning is easy stretch their capacities well beyond what is normally asked of them. There is no reason this can't be the experience of all teachers and the students they so want to help be their best—and whose best is required to help fix our troubled world.

—Philip Yenawine
Wellfleet, Massachusetts

CHAPTER 1

Permission to Wonder

LIKE MOST KIDS AT FOUR AND FIVE, my granddaughter, Wyla, made full use of "why"—from "Why is that car stopped?" to "Why is it raining?" One evening a year or so ago, it was "Why does that guy on the billboard look so weird?" She definitely expected her father and me to respond, and we did, but she didn't seem to pay a whole lot of attention to the answers we made up. She just kept repeating "why?"

Sound familiar?

If our answers didn't satisfy her, why did she keep asking? Why do so many children?

Maybe posing the question is the point. A child looks around her, and when she notices something she can't fathom, she asks about it. Our explanations don't suffice because, I believe, what she really wants from us is to know if it's okay to be puzzled and curious. She wants *permission to wonder.*

A LITTLE HISTORY

When I was running education programs at New York's Museum of Modern Art (MOMA), visitors also asked a lot of "why" questions about the complex, challenging, and often strange-looking art of the past hundred years or so. They wanted our team to explain what was unfamiliar to them, and we duly organized and crafted many explanations. But research showed that the ideas, facts, anecdotes, and analogies conveyed stuck with visitors about as well as our responses to Wyla.

After a great deal of thought—while digesting developmental research and theory by cognitive psychologist Abigail Housen and others—we realized the problem. What MOMA visitors really needed was what Wyla needs: not answers but permission to be puzzled and to think. Consent to use their powerful eyes and intelligent minds. Time to noodle and figure things out. The go-ahead to use what they already know to reflect on what they don't: the first steps in learning. Again, not answers but ways to figure out things on their own.

All of us have the capacity to engage with the unfamiliar. We do it often—for example, picture yourself in a city you've never visited. You're not going to leave your hotel totally bewildered. You'll look around, take in the scene, and head out, making sense of what catches your attention because of past experience. This is not to say you won't seek out maps and guides, but even without, you're not completely at sea. You start by using your own resources—exactly what any of us needs to do when we encounter art that strikes us as strange.

At MOMA, we needed a new strategy. We understood that the impetus for growth comes from curiosity—and our visitors, like Wyla, were plenty curious—but for them to grow, we needed to help them find the means to answer questions and solve problems themselves. By providing answers, we might have scratched the itch to know, but we were denying our visitors the opportunity to go through the effort involved in learning.

TEACHING THAT DIDN'T STICK

In 1987, roughly halfway through my time at MOMA, several trustees challenged my staff and me to find out if anyone learned from our many educational options. We were asked to be accountable for our teaching: were we effective? Did people learn what we taught? Sound familiar?

MOMA's education department offered a range of programs and materials to aid our visitors—most museums do—because surveys we conducted revealed that many wanted help. Museums have no mandated curriculum, but we offered standard tools of visitor education: teaching programs such as lectures, gallery talks, school group visits, teacher workshops, and so forth; an array of printed devices (e.g., labels and brochures); and audiovisual materials (such as introductory videos to exhibitions and interviews with artists).

These programs varied in terms of duration (from an hour to weeks) and targeted audience (from kids to scholars), but in most of them, we tried to explain why modern artists do the often-confusing things they do. We directed people's attention to details in images and objects, sometimes by way of questions, as we shared information and ideas interspersed with pertinent biographical stories and historical information. We offered analogies to help bridge the gap from what was familiar to a given audience to what was strange. We provided suggestions for looking that we hoped people could adopt and use when they encountered unfamiliar art. We sometimes included studio activities to help make certain points clear.

To all appearances, we did it well. Audiences were consistently responsive and enthusiastic. We could see their engagement. Evaluations were positive. Programs consistently filled.

Mission accomplished, it seemed.

That said, visitor evaluations didn't quite satisfy the MOMA trustees asked to help pick up the tab for our efforts. They prodded us to assess more deeply: "Visitors seem to like what you do, but does the teaching make any difference? Do people leave knowing more than when they came in?"

As we all know, those aren't easy questions to answer. Determining who learns what in schools remains challenging territory, despite decades of attention and many means of assessment. But we took the directive seriously and set ourselves the task of finding out. Given that testing visitors wasn't really an option, we turned to Abigail Housen, a cognitive psychologist who studies how people think when they look at art, and asked her to help us see if people retained what we taught them. She went to work gathering data about our teaching programs in particular.

To our surprise and great dismay, she found they *didn't* retain what we taught, even immediately after an experience. When visitors attending gallery talks, for example, were asked moments later to retrace their steps and relate what they remembered from the talk they'd just attended, they didn't even recall all the images examined, much less provide an accurate recounting of what they'd been told.

The news upset all of us, but perhaps me more profoundly than others: I wasn't interested in providing programs with no impact; teaching without learning wastes everyone's time and misses the point. I wanted what the trustees wanted: for our visitors to gain knowledge about the complicated objects artists devise—information visitors knew they didn't have and were motivated to learn. But even more, I wanted our visitors to get more pleasure and meaning from art. And I wanted such engagement to happen when people were on their own, not just when we were around to guide them.

I therefore took the failure to connect personally. I knew the value of art in my own life. Having regular, deep encounters with art seemed basic to my being. Interactions with it in many forms contributed profoundly to my feeling human, and I was discouraged to think our well-intended efforts fell short of helping others similarly engage.

WHY OUR TEACHING DIDN'T STICK

Abigail Housen figured out what was wrong. Housen is a scholar who did years of graduate study working alongside other brilliant people at Harvard University interested in how the mind develops. Her specific interest was in how viewers process what they see in art, a particularly rich and complicated way of thinking. In our efforts to find out what our audiences knew about art and what they learned from us, Housen's focus—thinking—turned us on to something ultimately more useful: not what they know, but how they use what they know.

This is an important distinction. Many tests reveal what information or skills have been taken in and committed to memory, at least for the short term. Too few measure the impact of knowing in action: what gets internalized and actually used over time, even outside the learning environment. Suppose we successfully memorize vocabulary, or dates, or mathematical formulas, and therefore pass the tests—do we actually use this acquired knowledge in our daily lives? Do we retain it months later? Do we apply what we've learned given related circumstances in the future? That was what Housen figured out how to study.

At the time we met, Housen had spent fifteen years observing and interviewing hundreds of viewers in order to understand their thinking as they process art. She developed a simple method to do so in 1978: having viewers talk out loud, in a free-form stream of consciousness, until they had nothing more to say. She transcribed these remarks, broke them into independent thoughts, classified them, and analyzed the patterns that emerged. When she grouped learners by thinking patterns, she was able to determine that people with different experience actually think differently, constituting distinct developmental stages. People with little contact with art apply what they know from their own lives to make sense of what they see. Experts also apply lived experience but add other ways of thinking: a variety of strategies as well as specific concepts and information acquired through lengthy effort.

From her studies of people with a wide range of experience, Housen knew that recall of information and/or skills at analyzing—essentially what we were trying to teach at MOMA—are only aspects of knowledge, not the whole picture. That was useful to acknowledge in itself: despite the value we place on information and analytical skill, they're not the be-all and end-all of knowledge.

I should have understood this already: my own connections to art are usually highly personal. I often fail to think about who made something or when and instead simply get drawn in by how a piece speaks to some not-particularly-analytical side of me. It's the same with reading: recognizing words and sentences is obviously necessary for literacy, but it's hardly all there is to getting the meaning from text. Being a good doctor involves a lot more than the command of facts. And many "uneducated" people know a whole lot about work, the world, and how to do things.

At some level we all know this, but still teaching—including ours at the museum where we had the freedom to chose what we taught—emphasizes this basically academic approach to teaching and learning.

That was a useful reminder, but what was actually shocking to us was Housen's assertion that these aspects of knowledge are basically irrelevant at the beginning stages of experience with art: even if introduced into teaching and apparently appreciated, they won't be internalized and redeployed. They can't be; the foundation isn't laid to contain such experience, so it just won't stick, or at least not firmly.

Fortunately, Housen also held the key to why people came to MOMA despite not "knowing" a great deal and even feeling somehow ill prepared: she knew that, as we look, what goes on in the minds of those she calls *beginning viewers* is satisfying even if they don't recognize a painter or style by name. Whether novice or expert, we can have a good time looking at art in our own way. What didn't help our beginning viewers were approaches like lectures and labels. While they would do fine making sense of images in their own ways, once the specter of specialized knowledge was revealed, they thought, "Oops. I guess I need to *know* something to have the right experience. Please help."

As Housen went to work helping us understand MOMA visitors, she used her research protocol[1] to get robust data and analyzed what she found in light of the insights her earlier work had revealed about various stages of development. By way of several studies, she found the large majority of visitors to be in early viewing stages. Even though they had contact with art during their lives, they spent little of it with "eyes on canvas" in Housen's words: looking deeply for an extended time and thinking about what they saw.

There's a slight irony here, which came to mind as a result of watching Wyla, that granddaughter of mine. Particularly when she was a toddler, she spent extended periods of time with her nose to the ground, watching bugs or whatever. We might call this her "eyes on canvas" time: she was having essential primary experience with the physical world. She looked upward at birds and saw planes and helicopters—she lives in Los Angeles—and *helicopter* ended up being one of her first words. And that's the point: having had the experience of noticing something, she connected a name with the thing, and it stuck. It remains stuck. Now at the ripe old age of six, she knows both the generic form of helicopters and differences between the types that crisscross the skies above her neighborhood. She spent time looking, became curious, listened to what was said, asked questions, and learned what was interesting to her. We've all seen some form of this with myriad kids. Why, then, does so little of the instruction we design reflect it?

Here's another irony: given the example of the lengthy, apparently riveting examinations of art objects that were part of our teaching, visitors didn't even pick up the habit of extended observation from our example, something innate in the likes of Wyla. Significantly, visitor studies at many museums reveal time and again that people glance at works for mere seconds, from which only the simplest impressions are possible. These same people wouldn't expect to understand a poem or story without reading it carefully—even rereading it—and then thinking about it. But they rarely applied that strategy to looking at art, not even after our teaching interventions.

When Housen applied her research tools to determine what our visitors retained from our programs—which facts and strategies they recalled and used—she found that those who turned to us for help were at a point where "learning to read" was the need, not being inundated with facts and ideas, no matter how intriguing. Meanwhile, Housen determined that our staff was at later stages of development; we had spent more time with art, were actually schooled in it, and spent our professional lives working with art and artists. As a consequence, we thought differently from our visitors. Our teaching made sense to us, but—although they could apparently take it in—our visitors couldn't retain it. It wasn't what they needed.

Our teaching was out of sync with what was developmentally reasonable. What an individual is capable of learning at any point is dependent on his (or her, of course; I go back and forth between the genders when I write) stage of development—just as when a child is learning to walk, she's not ready to skip. Partly because we were able "presenters," people could follow what we said and conveyed that they enjoyed the experience. But even though we gave people what they asked for and appreciated, it didn't stick. Interviews showed they remembered bits and snatches, but often out of context, and they even misunderstood much of what we said. They might, for example, recall that a particular Russian artist (Kasimir Malevich, as it happens) painted his precise geometric shapes by hand, without the aid of tape, but would still wonder why he'd bother to paint a white square on a white background. Or why we in the know considered it an earthshaking choice. And this in spite of our eloquence on just such issues . . .

Here's one way to think about our conundrum: our teaching seemed to engage audiences, but not enable them. Although attentive and appreciative, visitors still didn't learn viewing skills, facts, or ideas; we didn't even empower them to be keen observers.

This led to confusion: when you consistently command the attention of viewers, and when they praise and thank you for your efforts, it is hard to face that, when tested later, they retain little of what you taught.

Sadly, as too many of us know, the same thing happens every day throughout our educational system. Theoretically, K–12 education fosters sets of skills, provides a base of knowledge, and sends young people on to colleges or into the workforce prepared to undertake complicated tasks. But statistics tell us we succeed less often than we'd like; most performance assessments report that U.S. students' collective deficits in achievement and deficiencies are widely lamented by the people who want to hire them or who face them as college freshmen.

Teachers of myriad subjects confront this issue constantly: we teach; they don't learn, at least not enough. Most of us want to change that.

ENGAGEMENT: OUR ONE CONSISTENT PHENOMENON

One thing that was easy for us at MOMA was capturing the attention of our students. While that might be expected of adults—MOMA's grownup visitors came already interested (unless, of course, dragged by a date or mate)—it can't be said of the kids who were put on buses in schools and ended up in our galleries. Nonetheless, we had no problem getting or keeping their attention. Why?

First, we have the natural visual abilities of all sighted children and their innate habit of looking at what's around them. Like wondering Wyla, they examine things, faces, bugs, and the moon; thinking about this is a good reminder of the natural capacity of our eyes and minds. Think about how immigrant children figure out who's who and what's what in the absence of shared language; they do so by looking and thinking about what they see, testimony to the ubiquitous usefulness of vision.

Second, we have the nature of art. While we all are informed by innumerable images each day, little of it is categorized as art, a category apart from most imagery because of its complexity relative to, say, your average news photo or snapshot. Lots of what we see in art is common to daily experience, however. Art images depict people, places, things, expressions, interactions, moods, costumes, weather, spaces, light, colors: virtually all that we experience or imagine finds its way into art of various times and cultures. An important aspect of art is that feelings are embedded in it along with information, triggering a full range of responses from those who look at it thoughtfully.

Figure 1.1 shows an example from ancient Egypt that serves well to represent the qualities of art:[2]

Some of what we see here is familiar and recognizable, some mysterious, and most of it is both. It's not hard to recognize a number of human figures here, two of them probably adults; the one on the left is probably

Figure 1.1

male and the other female, but the genders are a little ambiguous. If they are a couple, then the smaller figures are very likely their children—at least it seems reasonable to infer as much because of the relaxed and familiar interactions. But exactly what's going on among them? The children look like small versions of the bigger people, but what rests on their heads might be different: are those crowns of some sort on the adults? The figures seem to have a lot of exposed skin, with only sandals for shoes. Are they inside or is it warm where they live? What might their garments be made of? Why are their faces, their profiles especially, so much alike? Many of us might recognize writing along the edges, and some might identify this as *hieroglyphics*, typical of Egyptian objects. But what does it say? A circle with lines (arrows?) pointing down from it is at the center of the top; is this the sun? Because the arrows seem to be directed at the figures, do they have some special relationship to the sun? The two adult figures rest their feet on pillows. Could this tell us something? What about the things that attach to the crowns—are they symbolic? If so, of what? Do the columns, only the right one of which is complete, stand for something? The lefthand corner seems to be missing a piece, but looking at it closely reminds us that this is a piece of stone, and the image is carved into it. The sides are chipped as well. What has happened to this piece over time to leave it in less than perfect shape?

See what I mean? Yes, we recognize and identify certain things, but that isn't the end of the story. Some of what makes us wonder might be answered by research, but can anyone say for sure what the relationships between the parents and kids are? Between the adults? They stare steadily at each other: does that say something? That's very likely an unanswerable question even for Egyptologists. But it's interesting to ponder anyway.

To keep us thinking about the nature of art, plenty of art contains depictions of a mother and child, but they are not all the same. One might convey us to a European church in the Middle Ages and another to an African village. They might be visually similar in most respects but quite different in the responses they evoke. Even two images of the Christian Madonna can come across differently: one formal, austere, and divine, and the other warm, maternal, and worldly.

The range of plausible interpretations for any work of art allows us much leeway; most of what we think, feel, and say can be justified if we take care and time to look, probe, and puzzle over what we see. We can find layers of meaning beneath what we think at first. Given time, we can recognize symbols and ponder metaphors.

It's tempting to say that art, especially if chosen pointedly for an audience, is inherently interesting. Many of its subjects have concerned humans for as long as we've bothered to make any kind of record. Most of it connects to deep strains within us. Perhaps the reason for the synergy between the arts and most religions is that, for a spiritual message to communicate, it must appeal to our hearts as much as our eyes and minds. The arts provide the means to do this, and when we are open and ready to experience it, we feed our spirits. There is something basic and human in this. The instinct to look, active since infancy, is well rewarded.

That said, in contemporary culture, art is, for the most part, found in museums and galleries. It is easy to live without seeing much of it beyond what we might choose to decorate our homes. This situation has helped create the impression that appreciating art requires special knowledge.

This separation of life and art was unthinkable in the not-too-distant past; what we collect in museums as art was often sacred and ceremonial in its original milieu, whether a painted Crucifixion or ritual masks from Native American people. The role of art has shifted in recent centuries from representing deeply held communal values to expressing the ideas and feelings of individual artists. Many artists, particularly the most innovative, work in relative isolation with little concern for the distance occurring between what they make and us "ordinary people." As a result, for many of us, while art may play a decorative role, a lot of what we find in museums exists in some other sphere, distinct from our lives. The result is what we saw at MOMA: even those predisposed to be interested in the art of our times feel the need for help with their encounters.

WORKING ON THE SOLUTION

Continuing to work with Housen, a team of MOMA staff set out to see if we could effectively teach what we came to call *viewing skills*—observing, interpreting what one sees, probing and reflecting on first and second thoughts, considering alternative meanings, and so on. Reflecting on this at some distance, it's easy to see something we didn't recognize at the time: we weren't *teaching* viewing skills. Both adults and children already have them. They simply need to be activated (or reactivated), honed, and directed.

Moreover, we had Housen's research. She had been able to identify for each viewing stage what might be termed "their questions."

For example, beginner viewers often try to create a narrative out of a picture. Their mode of processing can be phrased as "What is going on here?" When beginner viewers are asked this question, they are engaged because the question has a deep correspondence to the way they are predisposed to construct their ideas. The work that Housen and I later did together grew out of such constructivist assumptions.

Once we've ignited a process, it turns out that we can accomplish a whole lot more than art viewing. Given the combination of accessible information and elements of mystery, finding meaning in art is a form of problem solving; as we develop skills at viewing, we simultaneously learn how to find and solve problems. While the activity of examining art is not so different from a young person following a line of ants along the sidewalk to see where it leads, it is also how a scientist studies climate and a historian pieces together the past. What we need to start are eyes, memories, openness, time, and encouragement to engage in mind-stretching exploration—in other words, permission to wonder.

The method we developed to capitalize on all of this is called Visual Thinking Strategies (VTS), and it's now used in many museums. More germane to this book, it's implemented in many schools as a way not simply to integrate art, but also to teach young people how to dig into all sorts of unfamiliar material—stuff that might in fact come from cultures distant in time and whose languages are incomprehensible to us or from the realm of science—and we can start this with children before they read.

What MOMA visitors' questions revealed is that they needed to reconnect with how they learned as uninhibited children, something that schooling may in fact diminish. Dr. Diane Zimmerman—a veteran educator, writer, and retired superintendent from the Old Adobe Union School District (California)—summarizes her take on this:

Most teachers in the early grades believe in developmental learning. During the last decades, however, the emphasis has so shifted to text-based instruction, even in kindergarten, that we forget to capitalize on the natural ability of children to look, listen, and talk about their environment. By the time they enter school, children have demonstrated a natural ability to direct their learning toward what helps them make sense of the world. Children need to keep looking—and looking and talking—all through the middle years, a time of great cognitive creativity and drive. The brain has been primed to weave together all manner of learning to create deep understandings of the world. This developmental period signifies an emergence from dependency, with children becoming more independent while continuing to broaden their knowledge and skills. The ease of finding images, sounds, and videos on the Internet has opened a way for the teacher to bring this rich visual and auditory world, free of text, into the classroom and it's a mistake not to do it.

What and how children learn from life constitutes real and substantial skill and knowledge. We should acknowledge these as such, and continuously give kids the chance to use and widen their capacity to learn on their own. If we don't, we end up with adults who feel as if they need help understanding something well within their reach, as with our visitors at MOMA. For over twenty years, Abigail Housen and I led Visual Understanding in Education (VUE), a nonprofit organization that has implemented VTS and studied how looking and talking, facilitated by teachers, impacts cognition. Our intention, as you know, was to produce people, of all sorts and ages, who could find meaning and pleasure in works of art on their own. But it soon became bigger than that.

CHAPTER 2

Visual Thinking Strategies: The Basics

AN EARLY EXPERIMENT IN WHAT was to become Visual Thinking Strategies (VTS) was initiated with a stalwart group of New York City fifth-grade teachers in the fall of 1991. We decided to enlist teachers for several reasons: they were identical demographically to our adult audience at MOMA, but willing to work with us over an extended period of time and assist us with research. We could also study our teaching in two ways: using Abigail Housen's methods as well as watching the teachers apply what we taught them in their own classrooms. Housen and I presented them with a set of lessons to try while we—combining observations, Housen's protocol, and debriefings—studied the impact.

Here's an overview of VTS: the teacher facilitates a student-centered discovery process focused on carefully selected images. The teacher is central to the process but not the authoritative source; instead, the students drive the discussions, aided by the teacher. As facilitator, a VTS teacher helps students to:

- Look carefully at works of art
- Talk about what they observe
- Back up their ideas with evidence

- Listen to and consider the views of others
- Discuss and hold as possible a variety of interpretations

Our first group of teachers took to the process quickly and because of what we thought we could learn, it wasn't long before Housen and I began to concentrate our attention on work with schools rather than museums. While VTS is used in many museums as a tool for gallery teaching, a large number of them apply it in the context of their school partnerships for a reason we discovered almost immediately: the increased level of engagement. One quick and consistent report from the teachers was that virtually all students participated in VTS image discussions; it seemed to engage those who normally held back or whose attention wandered, and to erase distinctions applied to students— gifted or challenged, for example.

Since our first experiment in 1991, VTS has grown to become a K–6 curriculum used in schools across the United States and in some countries abroad; details regarding the curriculum are provided toward the end of this chapter. But to show why teachers respond to it, here's a typical example from many years later of what teachers first noticed and valued from Tracy McClure, a veteran sixth-grade teacher in Sonoma County, California. She made these notes in a journal describing a discussion that took place in her class when she introduced VTS to her students using figure 2.1:[1]

By the first lesson's second image, the conversation became particularly dynamic. A high status boy posited that even though the man and child in the picture had electric guitars, they were poor because the guitars weren't plugged into any source of electricity and because the girl wasn't wearing shoes. Other students agreed, building on the evidence of poverty by pointing out that the fencing was made of sticks, that the children in the background were wearing dirty clothing, and that the doorway didn't seem to harbor a solid door. At this point cognitive dissonance was on the verge of appearing. A student often isolated from peers on

Figure 2.1

the yard through teasing, stated, "I disagree that these people are poor. You can wear old and dirty clothes and go barefoot and still have enough money for the things you need. I think the reason their fence and house look the way they do is because they might be from another country or culture." I steeled myself for the abrasive criticism sure to come from the high status child or his peers. Magically, not one comment was voiced, not one set of eyes rolled, and not one gale of tormenting laughter burst forth. Instead, I saw heads nodding, foreheads furrowed in quizzical thought, and other hands raised. Another girl added on, inquiring, "Yeah, and what do we mean by poor anyway? Look how happy everyone seems. The girl is smiling and so is the taller kid in the background. And the man, who I think might be the dad, seems to be almost dancing when I look at the way his feet are. Even if they don't have much money, I don't think they are poor because they seem to be rich in the things that matter." My heart soared!

Many teachers have related such stories. And they've also told us something else extraordinary: that students apply skills learned in VTS discussions in other classes. Teachers identified the behaviors they saw as *critical thinking*, and noted students transferring some of this critical thinking—providing evidence, for example—to other lessons, something that is rare. (In a controlled study, Housen later showed that teachers were right: VTS increases various thinking skills that can transfer to another mode of inquiry.)

Housen had started our research simply wanting to see if we could build viewing skills and cause measurable change in thinking about art. In time, we recognized something bigger: the expansive power of the eye/mind connection and of talking about art as a way to jump-start many cognitive processes. Soon enough, following the insights of teachers, we began documenting the impact of VTS on writing. Eventually, as they had always done, teachers showed us how VTS could provide an avenue into teaching interactively in other subjects.

WHAT IS VTS?

I'm getting ahead of myself. Before we get into that, let's cover what VTS is.

Here's a way to describe it: VTS uses art to teach visual literacy, thinking, and communication skills—listening and expressing oneself. Growth is stimulated by several things:

- Looking at art of increasing complexity
- Answering developmentally based questions
- Participating in peer group discussions, carefully facilitated by teachers

To give you an idea of the process, consider the following excerpt from a discussion about figure 2.2[2] among fourth graders in their first year of VTS.

TEACHER: *All right, everyone, take a minute to look at this picture.*

TEACHER again, after a pause: *What's going on in this picture?*

STUDENT 1: *I think a poor family and there's a little daughter, and a dad and maybe the mom left and they're just living in this little tiny place. And that's why—I don't know if that's a little girl or boy—is crying. [As the student spoke, the teacher consistently pointed to all that was mentioned: the family, the dad, the child, the place.]*

TEACHER: *Okay, so you're looking at these figures and thinking they're a family. And that they're poor. Maybe the mother left them. What did you see that made you say they were poor?*

STUDENT 1: *Because they don't have, like, a very good house really. I think they're in that house. They don't have very good clothes either. Like their clothes are all wrecked up and ripped and the children's clothes are really dirty.*

TEACHER: *Okay, so you have several pieces of evidence that suggest they're poor to you. You're looking behind them, thinking they might live in a very plain house.*

Figure 2.2

And you're looking at their clothing and noticed that it's torn and soiled. All right, what more can we find?

STUDENT 2: *Um, I think that they're a poor family and maybe their mom died and maybe like something happened, so they're . . . And I also agree with Julian, I think that they live in a little place and maybe like a horrible storm happened.*

TEACHER: *Okay, you have a few ideas. You are also wondering about the mother. What did you see that made you say that something happened to her?*

STUDENT 2: *'Cause they're really upset and there's no mother in the picture.*

TEACHER: *Okay, so we're missing a mother figure and you see the others as upset about it. And what did you see that made you say they looked upset?*

STUDENT 2: *Because they're not, like, smiling and the little kid is, like, crying.*

TEACHER: *Okay, so you're looking at their facial expressions and sort of seeing that no one's smiling and this figure actually might even be crying. All right, what more can we find?*

STUDENT 3: *Well, I was thinking they are not poor, 'cause it doesn't matter what they look like. 'Cause they could have just finished, like, gardening and they are all just dirty from all the dirt. And the house, I just think it is a regular house, like all of our houses because, it is just showing part of the house.*

TEACHER: *Okay, so you're offering another interpretation, saying that people could be wearing clothes like this—sort of ripped and dirty—if they've been out gardening. Maybe we don't know everything about their situation.*

STUDENT 3: *Just because their clothes aren't good, doesn't mean they are poor.*

TEACHER: *So wearing worn clothes doesn't necessarily mean you're poor. Maybe they've been out working. And you were saying that we don't have a lot of information about where they are. It's just a little piece of the background and you are saying it could be any house. Okay, so it's another way to look at that. What more can we find?*

STUDENT 4: *I think they're poor and the mom did die and the son right there, he is really sad and he is crying. And the dad, he is like sad and angry that the mom died because maybe it wasn't a long time ago and they didn't really have that much to do and they need somebody to take care of the kids and cook. Well, and I think they own a small farm and the dad just, like, said something to the son to stop crying—"it's just your mom"—and the girl you could see that she's looking at the dad and it looks like she can't believe he said something like that.*

TEACHER: *Okay, so you're starting to imagine a whole story and some, almost like conversations or some thoughts that this group is having, and it all sort of revolves around the idea that the mom has died and they're left trying to work out what to do. And I'm just curious: what did you see that made you say that this figure might be crying?*

STUDENT 4: *Because he is holding his dad's arm and he's looking down like this.*

TEACHER: *Okay, so he's facing away and sort of burying his head and holding the father's arms. And this makes you think he might be really upset. What more?*

STUDENT 5: *I think it's really hard for them to live without the mother because the mother was really a big help, so now living is really hard. And also, I think behind the father's arm there is a bucket and I think they have to go down to a well to get water, so I think they're poor.*

TEACHER: *Okay, so you are agreeing with this idea that things are really hard because of the missing mother. Life has gotten much more difficult and they miss her. And here you've seen something we hadn't noticed, this shape, which might be bucket, which means they might have to get water from a well—another possible sign they have little money. What more can we find?*

STUDENT 6: *I don't think the mom died because she's not in the picture. She could be, like, in the house cleaning, in a different part of the house, or maybe making beds or something. Or maybe out in the garden or something.*

TEACHER: *Okay, so here's another possibility to explain why there's no woman in the picture . . .*

Somewhat abbreviated here, this conversation actually continued for another several minutes with more debate about the missing female figure, the subjects' economic condition, and the mood of the person they identify as the dad. But we see enough here to understand the role of the students as the ones who look, think, and talk about what they see, and the role of the teacher as a neutral facilitator of the process.

With the teacher basically standing aside to let the conversation develop as it will, individual students notice different things, contributing diverse observations, opinions, and pieces of information. The teacher accentuates the multiple possible interpretations by paraphrasing comments as if they were possibilities: *maybe* the family is poor, or this child *might be* crying. She also links answers, similarly stressing that any single interpretation is one of many possibilities. The group debates a few possible interpretations, applying what they know to figure out what's happening here. When time is up, no attempt is made to form a consensus regarding any of the interpretations entered into the discussion; the teacher thanks the students, usually compliments them on the seriousness of their efforts, and asks if they are ready for another image.

ANALYZING THE ELEMENTS OF VTS

Here's a summary of the process: first, the teacher projects a carefully chosen image and asks students to look at it quietly for a moment. Second, the teacher asks students to answer several specific but open-ended questions that come in sequence. She listens intently to what students say, pointing to what they mention and responding to each comment, paraphrasing every student's ideas. Finally, agreements and disagreements are linked while the teacher remains the facilitator throughout the discussion, not adding comments, correcting, or directing the students' attention. Typically the process takes fifteen to twenty minutes for each picture. Next, I'll discuss each element in some detail.

The Group

Having any discussion requires a group of people, and with this kind of subject matter, the group consists of enough sets of eyes and minds to make lots of observations and come up with different ideas and information. It's best if members of the group are peers: people—in this case, students—with different life experiences but who are similar in terms of developmental stage and/or knowledge of the subject. This is virtually guaranteed in most classrooms. With practice of VTS, teachers learn how to manage classes with thirty or more students or, occasionally, to break their classes into two for discussions.

A Subject to Discuss: Art

Art is the hook that engages students. It is selected in the same way that sensitive parents and educators choose books to appeal to their children. The subjects are familiar so that students have much to recognize, but they also contain elements of mystery so students have observations, ideas, and emotions to puzzle over. Subjects vary to make sure that a variety of student backgrounds and interests are called into play. Style and medium also vary: a diversity of visual vocabulary builds the sense that students can decode a range of images.

It's this combination of aspects—clearly readable information alongside ambiguity and diverse subjects and techniques—that makes art so useful in starting a deep and rigorous discovery process. Art is basic to VTS and the reason it makes such an impact on kids: they engage deeply with the images we carefully choose, and this engagement initiates an array of habits ranging from skill at observing to comfort in extracting meaning from complex problems. Once learned with art, the ability to learn from discussions carries over to other inquiries; VTS as a method is easily redeployed by teachers in other lessons.

Silent Looking: Asking Students to Look Before They Speak

Taking time to focus is rare in our contemporary world, but it's necessary if any subject is to be taken seriously. As teachers, we're often delighted to see many hands snap into the air, but at other times, it's wise to give students time to think before they speak. VTS provides one of those moments—and teachers usually allow less than a minute for this silent consideration of the image in question.

Good Questions

Carefully crafted questions set the students, stimulated to talk by the art, into an active discovery mode. The VTS questions in fact provide a beginning strategy—a structure—for examining and reasoning about any unfamiliar object. The specific questions as well as the phrasing of each are based on Housen's research:

- What's going on in this picture?
- What do you see that makes you say that?
- What more can we find?

The first question—*What's going on in this picture?*—initiates the inquiry into the meanings contained in the image: not just what's depicted but also what it conveys. The question's phrasing is familiar. We ask ourselves this question frequently. It is open-ended to suggest that all sorts of responses are acceptable. Still, it challenges students to move beyond observations to figuring out what they add up to. In fact, the wording encourages the finding of a narrative in the depiction, a meaning-making system supported by the art chosen and a behavior that Housen's data shows is within reach of students. While the first instinct might be to make a small number of random observations, the second impulse is to make sense of these observations by way of snippets of story. Debra Vigna, a second-grade teacher in Portland, Oregon, has observed that this impulse is so strong that if her kids encounter an image without a story, they complain it isn't a "real picture."

At first Housen and I thought that "What do you see in this picture?" was an equivalent question, but in fact we saw that it produces a less complicated way of thinking, appropriate for children of four and five years old at least to start, but not sufficiently challenging for older ones. One of the reasons this simpler question helps children still developing vocabulary is that it corresponds to what neuroscientists find about how the eye and mind work: the question engages a neuropathway in constant use, the connection between the parts of the brain that take in sensory perceptions and the brain's language centers.

The second question—*What do you see that makes you say that?*—is a nonthreatening way to introduce reasoning: students are asked to provide evidence of interpretations, staying anchored in the images. Even four- and five-year-olds can, after a short amount of time, demonstrate this remarkable thinking skill when the task is phrased this way. This also makes sense: they have been using their eyes and minds to reason since they figured out that just because one is small and frisky and another is big and lazy, both creatures are dogs. Or that a smile means one thing, a frown another.

The third question—*What more can we find?*—is asked often during VTS discussions and deepens the meaning-making process. Observing how long babies can stare at a single thing might remind us that the capacity to stay focused is operative in infancy and early childhood, and with this question we simply reawaken a behavior that is innate. While people bemoan the short attention spans of children (and perhaps the occasional grownup), what VTS teachers see is that, given something worthwhile to examine and pertinent prompts to follow, students will examine a subject for longer than most teachers have time.

Repeated use of this question also reinforces the notion that no matter how quickly we think we grasp something, further observing and reflecting often enlarges or changes first thoughts. Kids who have dissenting views, often extremely insightful, are encouraged to share them as well, affecting social dynamics in the classroom as well as divergent thinking. (Remember the discussion Tracy McClure wrote about where a high-functioning kid, inclined to put down others, was countered by one who was frequently subject to the first boy's attacks? And, to Tracy's delight, there was no negative result?)

The questions and their specific phrasing result from studying behaviors that appear in Housen's empirical data. Because she studied thinking, Housen has described specific patterns common to beginning viewers, and with these questions we simply ask people to do what naturally interests them. Originally we had additional questions or variations but, again, the field research indicated which to use. Debra Vigna, the second-grade teacher cited earlier, gives insight into the kind of data we accumulated in class after class, reporting that "When I tried asking my class 'What *else* can you find?' they shut down. They thought I was asking them to find something specific that they weren't mentioning. When I went back to 'What *more* can you find?' they opened back up."

We ask teachers to repeat the questions consistently so that students get used to them, recognize them, and begin to incorporate them into their own process. That is the point: we want the questions to lead to cognitive habits that stick. Data shows us that this happens, and once it does, students have learned a strategy for making meaning of art as well as other material unfamiliar to them.

When I was interviewing teachers for this book, a number made a point well stated by Rachel Zender, who teaches sixth grade in Spokane, Washington: "The teacher's understanding and knowing the questions is essential: when they haven't been memorized and the teacher seems to be trying to remember what's next, the discussions can feel forced and unnatural for the kids. Once I really had them down, I always knew what to do next, and I was free to be more present and the kids could see that."

Facilitation: Responding to Student Comments

In addition to asking questions, teachers facilitate the discussions: they point to the observed details and respond verbally to all comments, paraphrasing each comment and linking one comment to others.

POINTING. By *pointing*, quite literally, to what is observed in the image, teachers ensure that they know what a child is talking about and that everyone else sees it too, keeping eyes focused on the subject of discussion. Diane Zimmerman, the former superintendent and teacher, refers to pointing as *visual paraphrasing*: kids know you see what they do, and if you don't, can correct you.

In addition, pointing out one child's observation draws others' eyes to a spot another might have missed, and gives everyone a chance to discover more while there. For those learning English, it anchors words with images, a powerful way to increase vocabulary. (While just briefly mentioned here, this is a big topic in itself often commented upon by teachers of English as a second language. They find the whole VTS process an efficient means of helping kids build both competency and confidence. I return to this discovery in chapters 3 and 4.)

PARAPHRASING. By *paraphrasing*, the teacher is asked to accurately rephrase each comment. This has many implications beginning with indicating that the teacher has not just *heard* (repeating would prove that) but also *understands* what's been said.

Related to active listening, paraphrasing is a way of saying, "I hear what you say and understand it well enough to put it into my own words." Linda Sugano, who teaches fourth grade also in Spokane, describes paraphrasing as a way "of showing that you really grasp what someone has said and actually of honoring them"—something that she says has even had an impact on faculty interactions at her school where VTS is taught in all grades. In order to paraphrase, "the teacher must pay very close attention to all that is said, signaling that listening to others is important and providing a model of why: it helps you understand better."

The importance of feeling understood cannot be overstated, and I suspect all of us know kids (and perhaps the occasional adult) who feel no one understands them. By taking the time to listen and to reflect back what a student says, teachers build all students' sense of being valued and capable, a key ingredient in their ability to learn. Moreover, when students feel that the teacher understands everyone and treats all students equally, the playing field evens out and risk of speaking up is reduced. Paraphrasing also ensures something quite practical: that all in the group can hear each comment, which is sometimes difficult in a large class.

Meanwhile, paraphrasing is one reason VTS assists language development. If the teacher is careful and skillful, she can turn a student's halting answer into something crisper, clearer, or more exact. She helps him expand vocabulary, improve grammar, and/or increase the accuracy of language, but, importantly, students don't feel corrected; they feel smart hearing their idea expressed in the teacher's words. For example, a student comment taken from the earlier sample discussion went from "their clothes are all wrecked up and ripped and the children's clothes are really dirty" to "you're looking at their clothing and noticed that it's torn and soiled" when paraphrased by the teacher. (You often see the impact in kids' faces; they seem to be thinking, "Yes! That's what I meant!") The teacher didn't correct the student, but simply supplied another way to express what she heard. She demonstrated the possibilities inherent in rich vocabulary and simpler syntax, modeling thoughtful language use in the same way she modeled respectful listening. She's teaching indirectly, by pertinent example.

She was also careful about another aspect of her responses: most of the time she paraphrased a comment using conditional language, no matter how certain students were of the fact of their statements. She does this to underscore the aspect of art, and much else, that isn't black and white but open to interpretation. She's trying to encourage the thinking behavior of wondering, something left out of much assigned work in school where right answers are the objective. In these discussions, teachers can nurture the awareness and acceptability that many problems can be seen many ways and have many possible solutions. Few real-world problems are simple enough to be seen or addressed from one vantage point.

LINKING. By pointing and paraphrasing, teachers indicate that individual contributions matter; by *linking* answers, they show how ideas interact, making sense of a conversation that otherwise might seem random. By connecting ideas that agree, teachers make it clear that drawing the same or similar conclusions is often appropriate: "It seems that several people see that." By linking ideas that disagree, they indicate equally clearly that it's also possible for different people to respond differently to something they see: "We have a variety of opinions here."

Linking also shows how initial observations and inferences lead to others. For example, the teacher in the previous lesson linked comments in a strain of thought by saying: "You also point out the missing female but think she might just be in the house doing something." Linking outlines how early thoughts are probed, elaborated, and reconsidered, how new details add shades of meaning. It demonstrates too that listening to one another makes a difference, that in conversations all of us can and do build on the observations and knowledge of others, and sometimes even change our minds based on others' opinions or the information they contribute. No matter how ideas spill out, through linking the teacher attempts to keep track of disparate-seeming comments, acknowledging the cumulative benefits of thoughtful, reflective dialogue.

If teachers *maintain a neutral stance* throughout—never showing their own bias—important concepts are communicated, such as that you don't always need a teacher or an authority to help you figure things out. By letting the students go through their own process, they learn how knowledge is created: that it's not simply "delivered" by a teacher, parent, or media. They learn to think things through on their own, and find that they can rely on their peers for help, letting different ideas provide stimulation and different knowledge get factored in. Meanwhile, they come to realize that scrutiny and debate of ideas provide valid ways of testing hypotheses. This way, disagreement becomes interesting and valuable, not threatening, and most problems suggest not one solution but many or at least multifaceted answers.

Deferring again to Diane Zimmerman's ways of describing what she saw during several years of VTS implemented in her semirural district, she assesses that children become capable of "nuanced thinking." To her, the process "scaffolds deep learning." Think of it this way: if all

children left elementary school aware that most matters are complicated (not right or wrong, or black or white), that there are many ways
to think about most phenomena, and that there are usually multiple
solutions to problems, they would have learned essential twenty-first-
century skills for use in higher education and the workplace, directly
addressing the overarching goals of the Common Core standards.

Closing: Ending a Lesson

After initial discussions, some students ask "Did we get it right?" assuming, from past experience, that the teacher knows "the answer." But
they quickly get over this concern if the teacher maintains the stance
that this isn't about right and wrong but about thinking, and indicates,
through paraphrasing and linking, that the students singly and together
are capable of wonderful, grounded ideas.

Teachers often feel the need to provide closure to activities under-
taken in the classroom because it isn't immediately apparent to students
why an exercise was necessary. For the most part, this isn't the case
with VTS. Student discussions are authentic explorations of serious
topics—versions, in fact, of what experts do. Trying to summarize such
free-ranging discussions inevitably leaves out some of the commentary,
and all the good work valuing each answer can be undermined. Summaries are also superfluous; linking has already accomplished the job
of indicating the progress and value of the students' efforts.

After roughly twenty minutes of discussion, hands are usually
still in the air, and certainly once students are over suspicion that the
teacher is withholding information, they know they have fairly and
seriously examined, digested, and probed a challenging subject. And
they *still* have more to say.

VTS conversations therefore most appropriately end with a "thank
you" and ideally a comment about something we as teachers learned
from listening: "I was excited to hear how many details you noticed in
this image, more than I had," for example. Although Housen is dubious

about this, in the later elementary grades, a way of drawing things together after a series of lessons is to give students an opportunity to reflect on the purposes of VTS by asking, "What do you think you learn from image discussions?" While any student alone might be stumped by that question (Housen's worry), the collective mind can come up with substantial insights.

PRACTICAL DETAILS

With slight variations to accommodate different grade levels, the VTS curriculum consists of ten lessons for each grade spread over a school year beginning in prekindergarten and extending through fifth grade; it will soon extend through sixth. Each takes about an hour; the modest time commitment of VTS is intentional given all that teachers are expected to accomplish. We also found through research that the desired learning had "stuck" within this amount of time.

The pattern of teaching—the questions, the teacher's responses—is repeated from lesson to lesson to allow students a chance to assimilate the strategy. Each lesson involves two or three related but distinct images. The images are purposefully sequenced to become more complex over time. The roughly hour-long lessons are conducted once a month to allow time for what happens in each class to sink in; Housen refers to this as *incubation*.

Led by Housen, an extensive, iterative research process informed the selection of questions, the art, the number of lessons, and the spacing. Although VTS is often taught by specialists in various areas from English language learning (ELL) to art to special needs, it is best taught by the classroom generalist because of the shared experience it gives students and teacher, something that spills over into other lessons, as you will see in chapter 3.

The elementary curriculum spans all grades. Ideally, students in grades three and above get a museum visit toward the end of each year to make it obvious how skilled both students and teachers have become at negotiating new material even in an environment unfamiliar to many.

The basic elements of VTS are repeated year after year, but as students progress through the grades, gaining experience and growing continuously, we introduce additional questions, more challenging art, and new tasks like small-group work. We do so at moments when, according to data Housen collected by way of her interview research protocol, students need another prompt to keep moving ahead.

Although we are in the process of validating this approach in research studies, we have designed a curriculum in which sixth-grade students probe many works by artists they choose to study. By then, they are ready to push beyond what they can figure out on their own or as a group, and the lessons call for small groups to form around an artist they want to know more about; our image base supplies many options. In their groups, students first brainstorm questions and decide which to pursue, and then seek answers. This research usually takes time both in and out of class, and makes use of computers and the Internet to seek information and prepare presentations to share findings with others.[3]

In middle and high school, VTS is introduced as a discussion method, not a curriculum. The method remains essentially the same, although the art is different. The outcomes depend on the number of discussions conducted. This topic, however, is complex enough to merit its own text; this book deals almost exclusively with what we've learned from working with elementary schools.[4]

VTS: THE CHALLENGE TO TEACHERS

If we think back to the extended classroom transcript example included earlier, the teacher facilitated the discussion about the photograph of the family but did not direct it. She contributed no information. She refrained from "correcting." Instead, she echoed what the students observed, paraphrased their interpretations, and cited the evidence they supplied to back up their ideas. She let students make whatever observations they discovered and sort out among themselves what they thought was plausible. In so doing, she might have felt as if she missed "teachable moments" that she might ordinarily fill in by providing a fact, correcting a mistake, or pressing students to revise an idea or pursue a direction that seemed promising.

Why didn't she? Why not intervene? What if she had introduced a vocabulary word like *photography* or added some historical information—mentioned the Depression, for example (the era the photograph was taken to document)? What would be wrong with that?

Here are three quick answers: first, think of this as the start of a process, not the finish. We chose this image because it is an emotionally charged family portrait with kids as a central focus; it plays to students' interests in families and family dynamics. In this context, it is secondarily a historical document. Once kids are interested in it because of the characters and the story, a teacher can always return to it as a way of illustrating life at a particular time. If and when it is reintroduced, given the interest nurtured by VTS, students are likely to appreciate the way such images enliven and flesh out history that can otherwise seem abstract.

Second, while teachers are required to do a lot of direct instruction, this is a chance to let students explore a complex subject without direction. Instead of thinking about what's missing, it's not inappropriate to let yourself be excited about students' enthusiasm for discovering and sharing; they're doing that well. Independent thinking, collaboration, listening: these are things we can't "teach"; they have to be learned by other means, and VTS has proved to be one of those.

And, third, we might assess this kind of experience in terms of what we learned at MOMA: we supplied information routinely, and it didn't stick.

As Housen often points out, what viewers don't talk about, however important to us, isn't "their question." In this case, the students are busy probing the image for meaning, not medium or history. Why imply that they're missing something? Why dampen their willingness for and pleasure at talking about what interests them? Why limit thinking? Sure, the people are actually poor, but the kids' discussion lands on a pretty important point in itself: don't make assumptions or judgments based on circumstantial evidence.

The most important reason for this teacher's restraint is that, for this hour, her priority is to teach *thinking*. She took advantage of the open-ended nature of art to prioritize students' thinking and sharing ideas instead of finding right answers. She asked questions that ensure a certain rigor to the discussion. She didn't relinquish an active role, prompting students, for example, to supply evidence to back up observations and ideas. She facilitated in such a way as to stress respectful, extended examination and dialogue—collaborative peer interaction. But she let the students do the thinking, independent of her.

For thinking to develop, it's essential to have both a strategy for teaching it as well as an opportunity for young people to exercise their brains. By remaining the neutral facilitator, we are actually teaching students how to learn.

Significantly, the exchange among the kids is not unlike an advanced research team trying to find the solution to a problem. Scientists collaborate with regard to a particular subject, converse, bounce ideas off each other, ground opinions in evidence, consider options, and build on the knowledge and ideas of others as a way of achieving more than any individual could alone. They use these interactions as the basis for sorting out what they know and deciding what more they need to learn. Students gain experience in a very similar process and, usefully, it's free of the anxiety about right and wrong that often holds back many from participating.

IMPACT OF VTS: TEACHER COMMENTS

Here's what first-grade teacher Michael Gordon from Boston's Tobin School (where three-quarters of the students are Hispanic, most still learning English, and 86 percent of the students qualify for free or reduced lunch) wrote to me in an e-mail message describing the impact of VTS on his students:

> When I first began VTS with my first-grade students, they responded enthusiastically to the notion that we would be looking at art. Although my students read books or listen to stories with illustrations daily, they are interacting with the narrative of the text more than with the accompanying artwork or illustrations. VTS, however, provides them with opportunities to look solely at an image and react to it. The narrative is subject to one's interpretation. As I asked my students, 'What's going on in this picture?' they eagerly offered their own narratives. Moreover, I noticed that students who seldom participated during academic discussions were among the most animated hand-raisers during VTS. Students who struggled with reading or math and therefore might have shied away during those academic times were suddenly voicing their opinions about a piece of art. Perhaps they felt unburdened by the absence of text or comforted by the notion that there was no "right" answer.

Michael is typical of the teachers I asked to describe their experience with VTS. Tracy Madeiros, who teaches third grade at Tobin, said:

> First of all, VTS allows for an equal playing field. There is no wrong answer when observing, describing, and justifying what you see. This way all children feel comfortable, confident, and free to participate. They can express their thoughts and ideas in a safe situation and feel valued and supported.

Second-grade teacher Heather Sutherland heard about VTS from a family friend who worked at the Northwest Museum of Art and Culture in Spokane, Washington. Being drawn to art, she was intrigued from the start, but when she watched a video showing kids engaging in serious and thoughtful conversations, some of them on their own, Heather thought that VTS wouldn't just be great for kids: "It was something teachers would enjoy and might build community within the school as we learned to use it," which was a stated goal of her visionary principal at Garfield Elementary School, Clinton Price. Heather is now a several-year veteran of using VTS, and given that experience she reports:

VTS is a fantastic way to help kids go deeper with their thinking, can be utilized across content areas, is doable, and has benefits worth every second we spend on it. The things you see in students with writing, read-ing, [and] science justify the time. The dialogue and listening teaches kids how to be thoughtful citizens. I see them become more tolerant and flexible with each other, with me, and with their work. A real community builds among us.

These teachers have come to see VTS as an aid in preparing stu-dents to engage in the other work of school, a subject I'll discuss at length in the next chapter. At first glance, VTS can seem opposed to the direct instruction that marks most curricula in use, but my col-leagues in the classroom for the most part feel the different modes of teaching are complementary. For direct instruction to work, kids need to feel capable and up to the task of taking on complex material, a feeling easily resulting from VTS discussions. All students succeed, and the experience of success in one arena carries over to others. The thinking nurtured, and the related language ability, also transcend image lessons to make it easier for students to undertake challenges of other sorts.

Tracy McClure's sixth graders, with four years of VTS itself and also application of the strategy to discuss poetry, recognize this in their own way. In response to the question, "How do you learn best?" here are two typical answers from students:

I learn the best when I work in a group. I can really learn because I get more than one interpretation about something. Hearing my peers' inter-pretation of the subject might give me a new way of seeing or of solving something. I can't learn as much working alone or in pairs because I can't hear as many ways of thinking.

When I learn just about anything, I always like to hear people's ideas first and then I add on to them. I am the kind of person who has to talk through things in order to learn them. Another thing that I do when I learn is when I'm talking through it, I also get a picture in my head of what is going on in whatever I am learning at the time.

IN SUMMARY

When simply hoping to assist visitors at MOMA, we found a key unlocking much cognitive behavior relevant to schooling. Quickly learned, the pattern of questions sets in motion a strategy for making sense of anything unfamiliar. As students comment on what they see, they talk themselves into understandings of complex subject matter. The process gives them an extended chance to express their ideas, necessary for language development. It capitalizes on the fact that young people learn easily from each other.

In a significant way, VTS gives students confidence and clarity that, with the help of peers, they can comprehend what they encounter around them, learn from it, and move on from a grounded position. Over time, students learn how to readdress mistakes and blind alleys, to scrutinize a piece of information or an idea, rethink it, and discard or revise it as needed. They develop curiosity and want to know more. It's authentic life experience; it mirrors what experts do.

VTS gives young people permission to wonder, and more, the skills they need to begin addressing the issues that confront our global society.

CHAPTER 3

Applying VTS
to Other Subjects

WE WEREN'T LONG INTO our research testing the impact of VTS when some fifth graders turned *VTS* into a verb. A New York City teacher told us that her kids wanted "to VTS" the cover of a new chapter book they were about to start. She was willing and so asked them, "Well, *what do you think is going on here?*" Off they went. She felt that as a result of their discussion of the cover as well as a few illustrations, students read with more curiosity than usual and with a novel-but-welcome level of interest. They wanted to know if they had figured out the story from the pictures.

The teacher had a further reflection after the lesson: she thought that as a result of examining the images, students were able to visualize people, events, and locations in the story and that this had a positive impact on their comprehension of it. Consequently, she and the kids made "VTSing" all sorts of images a standard practice. We hear such anecdotes regularly to this day, and the teachers' impressions seem to resonate with what reading specialists say about comprehension: that understanding is aided by readers being able to visualize what they read.

Again during one of our early studies trying to find what thinking skills developed from VTS—this one in Byron, Minnesota—VTS project coordinator Catherine Egenberger noticed a second-grade classroom teacher asking her students to choose an image hanging on the wall and write about it as their visit to the Minneapolis Institute of Art was drawing to a close. Given their age and usual reluctance to write, the teacher thought it would be a quick exercise to fill a few minutes before meeting the bus to take them the two hours back to their small community in the farmlands of southeastern Minnesota. To her amazement, she actually had to pull the students away from what she thought would be simply a time killer. They were late for their bus, and while that was a problem for the driver, the teacher was intrigued—as were we. We began to watch for feedback that art as a prompt was an effective way to get kids to write. The feedback came and was consistent, so writing about images, usually after discussions, is now firmly entrenched as practice in most VTS classrooms.

That wasn't the end of what we learned from teachers, and this chapter relates some of it—how they came to apply the strategy to many subjects, a practice we never expected. VTS images engage more students more deeply than many other subjects, and many teachers are drawn to build on this enthusiasm by applying VTS as a teaching strategy in a variety of lessons. As previously noted, students, wanting "to VTS" images in texts, often lead teachers to this. The questions posed turn out to be the "right questions" for many different lessons and contexts for inquiry. Teachers who apply VTS to subjects other than art say it feels as if it were inevitable; they simply cannot resist extending the level playing field and the quality of participation into subjects where only some students traditionally succeed. When teachers see the impact, they make a conscious decision to apply VTS to aid learning in other subjects.

It's important to remember as you read ahead to some of these applications that applying the strategy to other lessons depends on it having been learned in the first place, something that data tells us happens because it starts with art. If directly applied to the cover of a book, for example, before the art experience, the conversation is so short as to be meaningless. The ability to make multiple observations and draw meaning from them depends on the experience students get by way of encounters with the richness of art. Anyone who tries to use VTS without the modest but essential experience with art finds it falls flat. It's not the fault of VTS but rather of the missing piece in students' learning. VUE has not conducted formal research to document the learning effects of the lessons described in this chapter; however, they are examples of VTS application that our training team has encountered as we worked to implement VTS in various settings.

VTS AND STANDARDIZED TESTS

VTS came of age as the era of "high stakes" testing dawned. While administrators became obsessed with scores, as they virtually have to do, teachers who were being asked to add a lot of test preparation to their teaching loads noted another phenomenon: VTS helped, it seemed, prepare kids for certain aspects of tests. Students developed the habit of supplying evidence during image discussions, and the skill carried over to test questions that required them to supply evidence, for example. Two research studies supported this observation.[1]

Perhaps even more important, however, to teachers who often look in vain for ways to engage their students, the VTS method—the questions, paraphrasing, linking—gave them a tool to get most of their students making discoveries together and sharing information and ideas as they dig into material that might at first look dull or formidable. The kids' experience discussing images gives them skills necessary to approach unfamiliar territory in a variety of lessons with enthusiasm and confidence. As more curricula ask kids not simply to arrive at the right answer but to show how they did it, the habit of talking things through, coming to understand them by way of explaining themselves, comes in handy. Whenever there is more than one way to express a problem, or more than one way to solve it, the multilayered thinking nurtured by VTS helps students noodle through the possibilities. This ability becomes more and more important in the era of the Common Core standards.

VTS: IMPLICATIONS AND USES

When I first met her, Elaine Chu was working at the New York–based foundation Open Society Institute (OSI), and because of her enthusiasm for VTS, OSI ended up sponsoring the early version of VTS in seven former Soviet nations. Over the course of several years, Elaine became so engaged with VTS that she eventually left OSI and joined our staff at VUE. In time her commitment to education became such that she decided to enroll in a masters-in-teaching program at Bank Street College of Education, after which she joined the faculty at the East Village Community School, a New York City public school where she taught third grade for six years. She currently teaches at a private school—the Little Red School House/Elisabeth Irwin, also in New York City—and when I asked her how she integrated VTS into her teaching, she wrote:

> *I'd say that I use the "strategies" for almost everything: asking students to make observations, connecting student ideas, identifying their thinking, asking for evidence. One thing that VTS did was help me approach math in an open-ended way, encouraging me to allow kids to share their problem solving approaches. Now, most teachers I know would say they do that, so maybe it's no big revelation. But I know that even when I thought I was listening to their ideas, I was still trying to direct them toward a particular way. I came to understand my role was to let them work through the problems, however inelegant they were sometimes, and to help them make sense of the material using their own strategies. VTS has also helped me to see the difference between authentic problems that are truly open-ended and allow multiple approaches versus those that are designed to teach a particular skill.*
>
> *Where I did abandon old approaches entirely was in social studies and resolving social conflicts in the classroom. A bullying incident my first year is perhaps most illustrative. After trying to discuss it with the kids (wherein they just gave the "right" answers), "reasoning" with kids, threatening,*

writing letters home to parents, [and] giving them time-outs at recess, all
to no avail, I finally turned over the problem to them and asked them to
first discuss what they noticed happening, not pushing a solution. One by
one the instigators admitted their part and came up with their own solu-
tions. I gave the problem back to the students, they owned it, stuck to their
solutions, and took pride in the change they were able to effect.

Even before Common Core standards started affecting classroom
practice, many teachers saw ways that VTS could help them reach more
kids at a deeper level than other forms of teaching seemed to do. Jeff
Rood, a second-grade teacher at the Laurelhurst School—a K–8 school
in Portland, Oregon, where VTS is in its fourth year—says that one of
his reasons for wanting to teach at Laurelhurst was VTS. He described
his interest to me in an e-mail message:

I have integrated the VTS strategies in all content areas of my teaching
within the classroom. I have been able to spontaneously experience a deep
understanding of how it is not the content of what is happening within the
teaching and learning environment, but rather the quality of what is hap-
pening, that provides advantages for learning and learners. VTS provides
a framework for engaging, implementing, and experiencing the complex
qualities that happen inside thinking and communicating.

Kimya Jackson was one of the teachers who made us realize that
VTS could be applied in ways we never imagined. For the past nine
of her twenty years teaching, she's been at the Redwood Elementary
School in West Orange, New Jersey, a town with varied terrain, some of
it high enough to have commanding views of Newark (five miles to the
east) and the New York City skyline (thirteen miles further). It retains
a small-town feel to some degree, with attractive houses from various
architectural periods in enclaves throughout the town, although it also
contains suburban development beginning in the post–World War II
housing boom. Redwood sits in a neighborhood of single-family homes

and tree-lined streets, bordered by a huge golf course and parkland. Its students reflect the diversity of West Orange, with roughly one-third Caucasian, one-third African American, and one-fifth Hispanic. Twenty-two percent of the students qualify for free or reduced lunch. Over 80 percent of the students in third grade test proficient in language arts.

After experiencing virtually all elementary grade levels, Kimya Jackson settled on teaching second grade, which she loves in part because "kids still have a thirst for learning but can tie their own shoes and blow their own noses." She is the kind of person who whips out her smartphone for instant translation when she and a student newly arrived from Ecuador get stuck. She teaches all subjects and reports that she "normally uses VTS as my anticipatory set. VTS gets my students thinking deeply about connections to the actual subject matter."

Kimya became a legend in VTS circles when we heard of her using the method to teach kids about nouns. Her first inspired stab at this involved her writing two lists of words on the board and asking what the students saw; she facilitated as they brainstormed their way to defining common and proper nouns. She later had a better idea. She did away with the lists, and simply wrote a lot of words on the board.

She first asks the students, "What do you see here?"—a question that simply asks for observations, and she gets simple answers in reply: "words," "things," "people's names." She ups the ante with, "What more can you find?" and the students burrow in more deeply: "names of places," "months," "titles of books we've read." When she adds, "What do you think is happening here?" they begin to make distinctions, reporting that some have capital letters, for example.

This discussion represents what she means by "anticipatory set," and it's basically a setup that results in the kids sorting the words into two categories that she then names for them: common and proper nouns. In a "think, pair, share" follow-up, students work together to figure out, word by word, which goes into which category, meanwhile learning how to define the differences and to decide when and how both forms are used.

With the same confidence in VTS—built over three years of using it in a straightforward manner with art—Marion Bageant says, "VTS works with anything that requires noticing, from examining dead bees to thinking about characters in a story." She has applied VTS in a variety of ways for the benefit of all students, but one inspiring aspect of her experience is how it affects students who are English language learners (ELLs) and those with severe learning challenges.

Seven years short of retirement, the effervescent and thoughtful Marion teaches second grade at Garfield Elementary School, which spans preK through sixth grade and is in Spokane, a city of roughly 210,000 people in the far eastern reaches of Washington State. Spokane is the commercial, banking, and entertainment hub of a large area once dominated by mining, lumbering, and agriculture, which still have a presence, but it is more diversified than it once was. Over 70 percent of Garfield's mostly white students require free or reduced meals, 22 percent of the students are in special education, and 7 percent are deemed "transitional bilingual." The school's test performance record has been improving steadily; Garfield was awarded a 2012 Washington State Achievement Award for closing achievement gaps. Marion believes that VTS has helped with this, creating a level field for all to play on.

VTS came to Garfield by way of an energetic, knowledgeable, and approachable educator at the Northwest Museum of Art, one of the city's cultural assets. Heidi Arbogast knew of VTS from its reputation within the museum community, undertook to learn it through a series of trainings, and has become one of the most effective VTS trainers working in the field. She became deeply involved because she decided that VTS could be the basis of partnership programs with Spokane schools, one that would build an empowered audience of teachers and young people for the museum and could also serve priorities at the schools in terms of literacy and thinking. Garfield Elementary was the first school in Spokane to respond to Heidi's overture, and the implementation began in 2008. A number of teachers at Garfield were kind enough to share insights with me to include in this book.

Virtually the first thing that burst out of the irrepressible Marion's mouth as she began to talk about her experience with VTS was its impact on listening, still a nascent behavior in most children in second grade, just as writing and math are also a struggle for most. But the importance of listening is hard to overestimate, perhaps especially when it comes to students still learning English.

Although her classes are usually full of kids referred to as "at risk"—the fathers of two were jailed, none were "advantaged" during one recent year—the students in Marion's second-grade class range from high achievers, ready for anything, to students who rarely contribute. It's rare for a single activity to engage the whole class at a high level. When they do VTS, however, all are "riveted" according to Marion. That said, they don't all contribute to the conversations equally. Some of her students typically hold back because of limited English and others because of severe challenges.

It's a truism to say that learning requires active participation, and in the instance of VTS, half the "doing" is talking. If, therefore, some students don't talk, do they learn as much as those who contribute? Marion is convinced that they do. During discussions, the activity may be happening in their heads, but this processing is substantial enough to show up in the writing she asks them to do afterward. She finds it to be replete with observations and ideas, commensurate with other students.

We will look at a variety of writing samples from Marion's ELL students in chapter 4 to see the evidence of her claim, but what seems germane here is the case of one particular student. Allen, as I'll call him, has been diagnosed with severe learning disabilities but cannot be on medication because of a health condition. Marion described him to me in an e-mail message:

He had difficulty staying on task past two minutes and could not focus to finish. He would be up, pacing the floor or having nervous tics when his attention waned. Even as of the middle of the school year, he called me "teacher" and not by my name. He also had difficulty engaging with other students and did not make eye contact with anyone. He had an Individualized Education Program (IEP) in reading and math. He also got layered intervention by me as well as my student teachers. I tried to support him with as many useful adults and activities as possible. He exhibited many of the behaviors of autism; however [he] had not been diagnosed with it. His older brother does have Tourette's Syndrome. His family is on free/reduced lunch and on the poverty spectrum.

During VTS discussions Allen tended to seek a spot in the front row and, uncharacteristically, paid close attention to the images and discussion. Afterward, Marion asked the students to choose one of the two images they'd discussed and write about it. Allen was unable to write, but Marion determined that he wanted to explain his thoughts if someone would write them down for him. By way of a scribe:

He spent twenty solid minutes explaining his ideas. He came up with complete descriptions, full of detail and thoughtful consideration of what he saw. It was a real breakthrough. He also, for the first time, felt engaged and a part of the classroom.

Marion's class observed a painting of antelopes and Native Americans on horseback; they seem to be fleeing a fire that burns bright red and low along the horizon. The smoke clouds billow dramatically in the sky, blown across the landscape—part gray, part black, and streaked with red. Along the front of the image, partially hidden by low plants, wolves seem to slink, perhaps slightly less interested in escaping than in taking an antelope with them. Allen described his view of the scene to a scribe:

The deer are hopping and jumping because I think there are dark clouds invading their worlds. The wolves are trying to camouflage so they can eat the people, horses, and deer. I know, because wolves eat. Everybody knows they eat anything. The flaming darkness helps the wolves

complete their mission teaching their babies how to hunt and the red
must be pieces of their soul—the wolves. Because the colors are mad
and red and I think the wolves are aliens because they are trying to cam-
ouflage. They go behind a bush and turn the exact same color.

What Allen "writes" may not be precisely what others might see, and the Native Americans are obliquely referred to as "people," but his description makes sense and his interpretation contains a plausible, coherent narrative. His choice of language comes close to poetic at various moments: "dark clouds invading their worlds," "flaming darkness helps the wolves complete their mission," "the colors are mad and red." He cannot communicate with others easily, but clearly he has a capacity for language; it's likely the combination of images and the experience of hearing images discussed that engages and enables him, with a small amount of additional help, to achieve remarkably. Afterward, he exultantly walked around the room exhibiting his writing accomplishment for his classmates to see.

VTS AND MATH: AN EXAMPLE

Marion dips into the reserve of experience her students have with periodic VTS discussions in a variety of lessons. Part of the second-grade math curriculum centers on story problems that deal with addition, subtraction, and unknown change. Marion recently decided to experiment with writing the story problem on paper affixed to an easel and assembled the kids around her. She posted the familiar VTS questions on a note clipped to the side. Here's an example of one of the word problems:

Problem with Unknown Change
Alden, Tony, and Dave were building snowmen at recess. They built _____ snowmen. Margie and Aaron came along and built more snowmen. Then they had _____ snowmen in all. How many did Margie and Aaron build?

She started the discussion with an open-ended question adapted from VTS, "What's going on in this story?" and then gave students time to focus on the meaning of the problem and to determine what they needed to find out. As they brainstormed what they knew, she made a bulleted record of their responses on the poster beneath the problem statement itself. After each response, Marion countered with, "What did you see that made you say that?"

For example, Adam offered an idea, "How many snowmen." To which Marion responded: "What do you see that makes you say that?"

"Because at the end they are asking that question and that's the most important thing we need to find out!" And, he added, "The snowmen are going to be less than the total number."

Marion was delighted, and told me:

Usually, I have to prompt students to think about whether the number is going to be less than or greater than the sum. In the past I would have done most of the talking. I would have had six steps, for example; circle the numbers, underline the questions, ask if it's a plus or minus, etc. A few would have gotten it, but many would not even know where to start.

But through this collective process, prompted by questions, building off one another, they figured out that by the time Margie and Aaron were finished (it must have been a pretty long recess and a great snowfall), they had more snowmen than the first three sculptors created.

Knowing that they actually understood the problem, Marion filled in two of the blanks with numbers, leaving one blank, and then asked the class, "What can you do now?"

Students soon offered one solution: "We could write out 'eleven plus _____ equals thirty-two.'" And then another: "We could write it, 'thirty-two minus eleven equals _____.'"

Marion wrote out both equations on the paper and again asked students to explain themselves, confirming that they could articulate this final step, giving more proof that they actually understood.

Once this group process was complete, students returned to their seats and solved the equations on their work sheets using either math tools or "mental math." Figure 3.1 shows several examples, all from ELL students who usually struggle most with word problems.[2]

The students were able to determine the missing number, but the point of the lesson was only partially about getting to the right answer. Marion's bigger intention was fundamentally constructivist: for students to be clear that they could figure out what the problem was asking and come up with a way—ideally, more than one—of solving it.

This problem is one of a set of story problems that constitutes a unit, and at the end of units, students are tested. Table 3.1 gives a comparison of scores after Unit 2 (taught according to her traditional means of explaining the problem and showing how to solve it) and Units 3, 6, and 7 (taught by way of discussions like the preceding one).

Marion downplayed the results, writing that they weren't "terribly huge, but a difference nonetheless. This proves to me the validity of discussing the problems in this open-ended way: because of the strong higher scores in general and number of students at Levels 3 and 4. The most dramatic change is among those who struggle most."

I would add this to her assessment: let's remember that all twenty-two students in the class were labeled "at risk." All of the math problems were stories. Allen, the special needs student we met earlier, scored at Level 3 in Unit 3, and remained there, though in addition to the discussion, he had the problems written into his IEP by an aide. Nevertheless, he solved the problems on his work sheets by himself. Another severely learning-challenged student had a perfect score in two of the following unit tests. In addition, two of five ELLs scored at Level 4 and two at Level 3 on the Unit 3 test, despite how they normally struggled with word-based problems. They continued to achieve at this level in the following tests. It's too soon to say that this learning will stick for longer than Marion might have expected in the past. Suffice it to say that the progress is wholly in the right direction, and Marion's willing to say that VTS-inspired discussion is the reason.

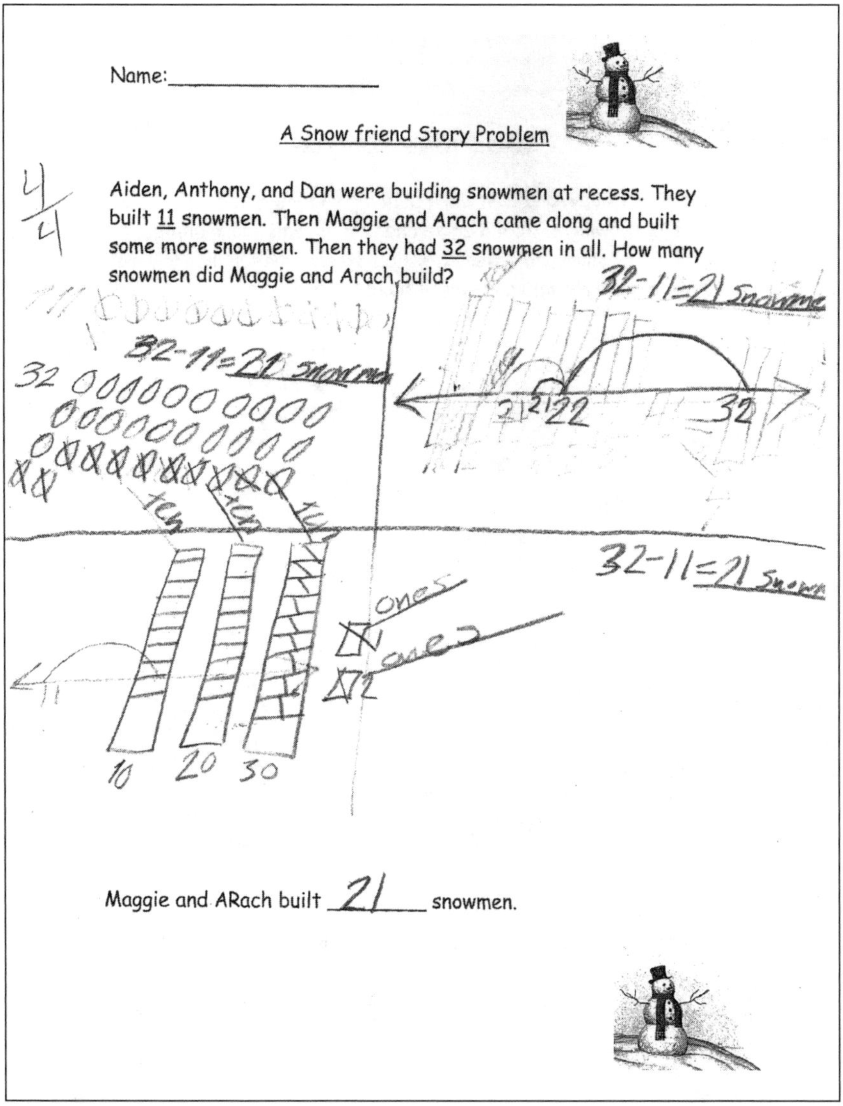

Name:_____

A Snow friend Story Problem

$\frac{4}{4}$

Aiden, Anthony, and Dan were building snowmen at recess. They built <u>11</u> snowmen. Then Maggie and Arach came along and built some more snowmen. Then they had <u>32</u> snowmen in all. How many snowmen did Maggie and Arach build?

32 - 11 = 21 Snowme

32 0000000000
0000000000
0 00000000
XX XXXXXXXX
ten   ten   ten

32 - 11 = 21 snow men

21 22 22   32

32 - 11 = 21 Snown

ones
ones

10   20   30

Maggie and ARach built ___21___ snowmen.

Figure 3.1a

Name:_____

A Snow friend Story Problem

Aiden, Anthony, and Dan were building snowmen at recess. They built 11 snowmen. Then Maggie and Arach came along and built some more snowmen. Then they had 32 snowmen in all. How many snowmen did Maggie and Arach build?

$\frac{4}{4}$

$$32 - 11 = 21$$

Maggie and ARach built ___21___ snowmen.

Figure 3.1b

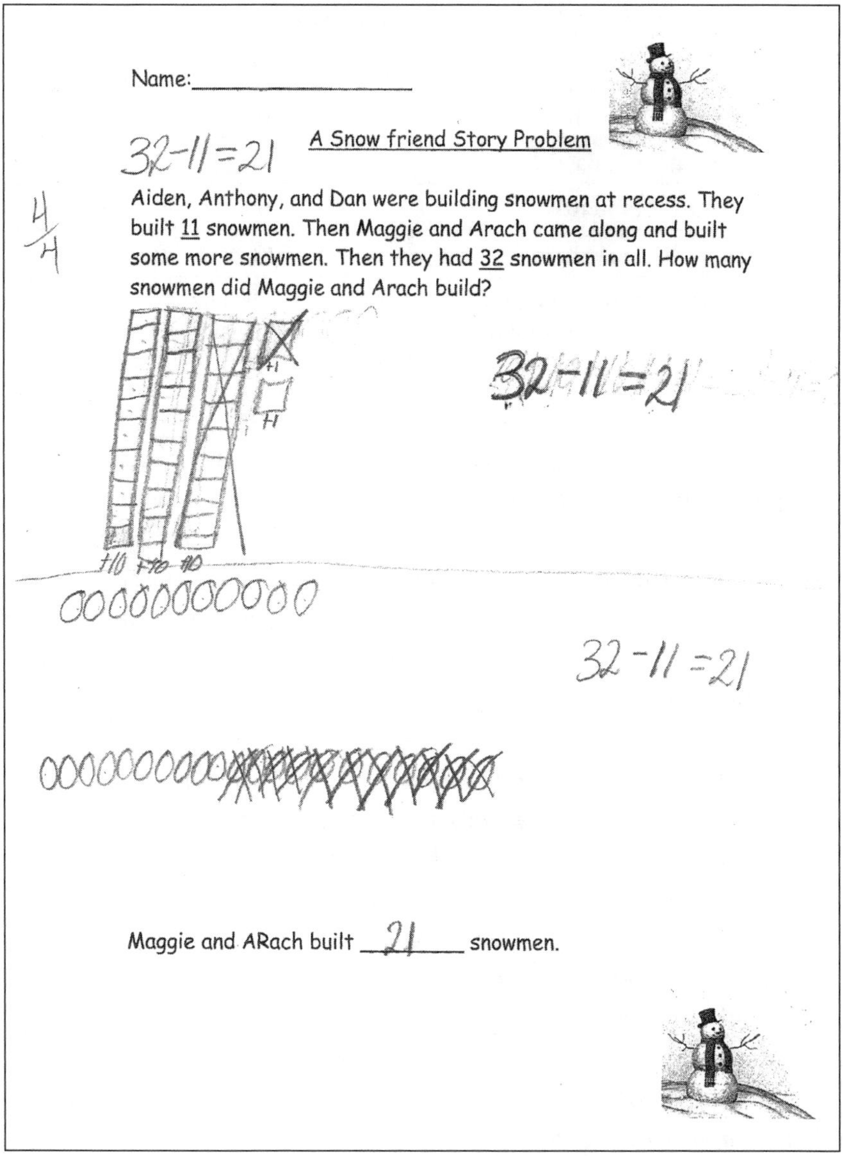

Name:_____

$32-11=21$ <u>A Snow friend Story Problem</u>

$\frac{4}{H}$

Aiden, Anthony, and Dan were building snowmen at recess. They built <u>11</u> snowmen. Then Maggie and Arach came along and built some more snowmen. Then they had <u>32</u> snowmen in all. How many snowmen did Maggie and Arach build?

$32-11=21$

+10 +10 +10

OOOOOOOOOOO

$32-11=21$

OOOOOOOOOOXXXXXXXXXX

Maggie and ARach built __21__ snowmen.

Figure 3.1c

Table 3.1   Math Unit Test Score Comparisons

	Unit 2[a]	Unit 3	Unit 6[b]	Unit 7
Level 1: Below Basic Standard	1	0	0	0
Level 2: Approaching Basic Standard	3	3	4	1
Level 3: Meeting Standard	13	6	9	17
Level 4: Exceeding Standard	5	13	8	4

a. Before the teacher, Marion Bageant, began having students talk their way through the word problems that constitute the third-grade math curriculum.
b. One student was absent the day of the unit test.

Marion basically operates as a field researcher in her classroom at this point. She makes tapes of lessons that she later studies with her colleague Heidi Arbogast from the Museum; they also coteach upon occasion so that they both can watch the students. Given the seriousness of these procedures, Marion's observations suggest a topic that might be studied in more extensive and formal ways. She wrote to me in an e-mail message:

> As I have been poring over my VTS lessons, notes, and tapes, I made a new and delightful discovery about my students. I think because of the combination of discussions in math and other subject[s] and the intensity of writing about images after every lesson, I have noticed my students using a skill that is hard to teach anyone, much less second graders. They are metacognitive of their thinking. I see that they are actually thinking about how to think. Providing evidence without being prompted and doing it naturally. Wow, big stuff for second graders. After the last lesson, one of my special needs students even said, "I wonder why I am thinking this way about this picture."

Even if the evidence is anecdotal at this point and only about this class, Marion's process is a form of formative research. As her observations stand, they describe capacities that most teaching and testing has ignored for the past fifteen years and now must be accomplished to meet Common Core standards.

VTS AND SOCIAL STUDIES: AN EXAMPLE

Many teachers integrate VTS questions and the facilitation method in almost unconscious ways when faced with students not understanding something important. With the concrete example of Marion Bageant's math story problem lesson, however, we see a decision made after several years of VTS seeping into her interactions with students. She very consciously chose to shift her approach to teaching actual curricular requirements in her second-grade class. Brian Fizer, too, started with VTS image discussions but has invented his own lessons, in part abandoning an existing social studies curriculum while still addressing the Massachusetts standards.

Brian quit a successful career in retail because something was missing from his life. He found himself wishing he had followed the impulse he had had in college—to become a teacher—which, for a variety of reasons, he had set aside for more than a decade. At some point it occurred to him it was time for a change, and he began to pursue what became as much a mission for him as it was a career: helping kids learn.

Brian set himself in motion by enrolling in graduate school at Northeastern University in Boston. While still taking classes, he was alerted by a classmate to an opening as a permanent substitute in the Tobin School, where she taught in nearby Roxbury—a neighborhood that by its own assertion serves as the heart of black culture in Boston. It is where Michael Gordon and Tracy Madeiros, heard from in chapter 2, teach. Almost 90 percent of the Tobin School's kids qualify for free or reduced lunch and a large percentage immigrated recently to the United States; over 70 percent of the students are Hispanic. The school struggles with test scores. It was exactly the kind of place where Brian wanted to commit himself.

Shortly after he began his tenure as a sub, Brian was offered a full-time position as a second-grade teacher. I interviewed him one summer day after I'd seen him teaching the third-grade class of English language learners now assigned to him, in his fifth year at Tobin.

When I started I was using what was assigned to us to teach, and it was eye opening. I had just finished theoretical readings assigned in grad school, and I saw that the mandated curriculum didn't resemble what I'd studied or the images I had of working with kids. But I didn't really know how to be a teacher at first, and I didn't know how to replace or improve on what I was given. But I did know the material wasn't exciting either to the kids or me, and I didn't like the interactions I was having with kids. Maybe even for selfish reasons, I wanted to have conversations with them. I learn so much about them from listening to them.

As it happened, the Isabella Stewart Gardner Museum education department, like the museum in Spokane, used VTS in its outreach to schools. During Brian's first year, it expanded a long-time partnership with the Tobin School to offer VTS professional development for the entire staff. "When I heard about VTS, I got interested," he went on.

Before training, I checked it out online. It matched my personality and the way I like to talk to kids. As soon as I started doing VTS I had insights into the language possibilities, particularly helpful in my class of ELL students. I also think the appeal was immediate because I could also see using questions to launch different lessons to give entry for a range of kids in my class, particularly with language and social studies.

He summarized the ensuing years this way:

By my third or fourth year of teaching, I became comfortable with finding my own resources, and with the fact that I could cover the standards in other than the prescribed ways. This is where VTS fits in.

I was witness to what he means by this when I went to visit his classroom in the spring of 2012. The social studies class I saw was actually a follow-up to one the preceding week, both addressing American history. According to Massachusetts social studies frameworks for second grade, "a history and social science curriculum should help students acquire a common understanding of American history, its political principles, and its system of government in order to prepare them for responsible participation in our schools and civic life." Despite the fact that kids at seven and eight years old are still working out the concept of time (as I see it, most think there is "now" and the "olden days"; I just read a seven-year-old's response to a painting made in 1635 as "from a long time ago . . . it was in twenty years"), the framework optimistically spells out the objective that students "learn world and United States history, geography, economics, and government."

In third grade—the grade Brian now taught—students are supposed to build on this, "drawing on information from local historic sites, historical societies, and museums . . . (to) learn about the history of Massachusetts from the time of the arrival of the Pilgrims" and "about famous people and events in Massachusetts' history."

This would be a tall order for eight-year-olds who have lived in Boston their whole lives, but since most of Brian's students arrived from other countries as recently as the year before and are still working to learn English, the challenge to achieve the standards is even more intense. I was extremely interested to see how Brian applied VTS to help him in this regard.

In class the preceding week, Brian projected a slide he made of the Bill of Rights—the first ten amendments to the U.S. Constitution—and he pointed to each amendment, one by one, often phrase by phrase, asking the students, "What's going on here?" They knew the drill from their VTS image lessons, and collectively they brainstormed the focus of each amendment. Remember: we're talking about third graders, and here's the content of the first amendment:

Congress shall make no law respecting an establishment of religion, or prohibiting the free exercise thereof; or abridging the freedom of speech, or of the press; or the right of the people peaceably to assemble, and to petition the Government for a redress of grievances.

It takes some figuring out merely to understand the wording, let alone each of the matters protected. With Brian facilitating by paraphrasing each comment and linking various ideas, however, the kids collectively did this figuring. Brian helped them shape their thoughts but didn't add information any more than he does during image discussions; the kids did the work of ferreting out the issues the amendments were created to protect.

They reasoned that this amendment protected several rights, and Brian helped them to sort out and clarify what these were by two means: judicious use of "What did you read that makes you say that?" and adroit paraphrasing with vocabulary that helped them understand words such as *abridging* and phrases such as "peaceably to assemble" and "redress of grievances."

Let's put this in perspective. The experience many of us have had, like me at MOMA, is that it's hard to teach many facts and ideas in ways that stick and are remembered and internalized, especially when the audience has little preparation and no choice about what it's supposed to learn, and the desired learning is at the far reaches of what is possible developmentally. It's hard even to engage, much less intrigue, much less enable learning in this context. Such teaching is complicated in schools because much of what we're told kids must learn in social studies and science ends up being presented quickly. The teaching is little enhanced by textbooks that—even though jam-packed with pictures, maps, charts, and the like—are rarely engaging. That said, if approached in certain ways, the meat of history, even that as seemingly dry (and perhaps only remotely relevant to children) as constitutional amendments, can become pertinent and understood.

What Brian observed was that his students grasped difficult concepts expressed in arcane language when given the chance to noodle through them in their own ways. His third graders are capable of handling the requirements of the Massachusetts frameworks if invited to explore the material actively and in their own terms. Of course, a facilitating teacher is necessary to provide assists by listening, helping students frame their thoughts, and making sure the process is rigorous and thorough. But once these young people had grappled with the first amendment, they moved on to the next, and then the remaining eight.

It took about an hour, after which Brian said, "Now that we've seen this Bill of Rights, imagine you are establishing a new nation. What sort of things would you include among the nonnegotiable rights?" Working in pairs, students were given the task of devising lists of matters they thought merited protection.

"Within about thirty minutes, they came up with great ones," he told me in a recent e-mail message.

Here's what I remember: Everyone has health care. Everyone has the right to happiness. Everyone has the right to marry or not as they see fit (some explicitly spelled out gay marriage). Everyone has a right to speak his or her own language. Everyone has the right to shelter, to work, to be protected from poverty. Everyone has the right to education and to be safe.

The third graders had come up with powerful lists of rights. No single pair of kids came up with all of the aforementioned ideas, of course, and they generated some of them during the follow-up process of comparing lists, again facilitated by Brian. But it seems they had learned at least several points effectively: that the government has a role in protecting people in certain ways; that there were certain "rights" shared by all citizens; and that some of these are spelled out and appended to the Constitution. Perhaps most importantly, I suspect they took away from this a sense that looking into the past is not just to learn about "the olden days" but to see what we can learn from past actions to apply now. The kids' list reflects their perceptions that certain matters of importance remain unprotected today. I don't know when I had a grasp of such issues, but I'm pretty sure I was older than eight.

In order to apply VTS in this way, Brian changes only a couple of words. For the first question he asked, "What's going on in this text?" and when the second is needed, he asks, "What did you read that makes you say that?" He responds to comments exactly as he does during the ten VTS image discussions each year. Because of these, he has two things to count on when he applies VTS to a different subject matter: his students' familiarity with the questions and the facilitated brainstorming process generally, and the confidence they have in collaborative meaning making. Kids in Brian's class, at least those who haven't come more recently to this country, have had VTS in kindergarten, first, and second grades, and the cumulative experience equips them to engage with unfamiliar material having the sense that collectively they can figure it out. After their discussions in the class I observed, the kids, again in pairs, wrote up laws they would see fit to enact.

After visiting Brian's class, I was reminded of a VTS social studies/current events experiment of my own. I conducted a VTS-style discussion among sixth graders using a combination of maps, news stories, and photographs taken from the *New York Times* of a military standoff between Israelis and Palestinians in the Gaza Strip in January 2009—a subject, it turned out, the students knew nothing about. I found this out by reading aloud the first phrase of the news article summarizing the clash: "The Gaza Strip lies along the Mediterranean coast." The name *Gaza* meant nothing to anyone, and to the extent that one boy recognized the Mediterranean it was, maybe, "an ocean?"

At this point I clicked on a slide that contained a map of the area. "What's going on here?" I asked, and they located Gaza, Israel, the Mediterranean, Egypt, various landmarks having to do with the recent conflict, and so forth. With this in their minds, we proceeded to go back and forth between text and five news photographs that showed fighting and the destruction left in its wake. The story told in the text was made real by way of the images. Tracy McClure—from whom we've already heard and who teaches at Old Adobe, where I was guest-teaching this lesson—offers her account:

*The students were fearless in their search for meaning about events oc-
curring in a place of which most had never heard, much less had any
sense of why. Students were totally focused, and their entire meaning
making was based on evidence from the text and images. After a lengthy
discussion, lasting over an hour and a half and spilling into the lunch
period, students wrote what they had learned and recorded any questions they had.*

*Some of these questions were quite profound: Why did the UN re-
locate the Israelis to the center of Arabic territory? Why are the Israelis
and the Hamas still fighting if it's not solving the problem? Why can't
they set aside their differences? What is a terrorist? Do the Palestinians
consider other groups as terrorists? Since it won't solve anything, why are
they killing innocent people, instead of the people responsible? How is
the United States helping the Israelis and why? If they are fighting over
land, why are they destroying it?*

Admittedly, these sixth graders simplified a very complex situation, but I thought, somewhat sadly, leave it to children to cut through
to core truths. I wished their common sense ruled the affairs of adults.

Tracy came up with the final part of this lesson: for the students
to take the article and images home to their parents and brief them on
their discussion. "While debriefing the homework," Tracy wrote to me,
"students shared articles their parents found helpful in understanding
the topic, revealed that their parents had questions similar to their own,
and added information about the culture of the area."

When applied to documentary material, VTS not only provides a
means to learn from primary source material but also gives insight into
how historians and anthropologists themselves work—by making careful observations and drawing conclusions from them based in evidence,
which is in fact not much different from how scientists work. As students
"VTS" microscopic images or satellite photos of weather systems, for
example, they gain a window into how scientists approach complicated
subjects, enabling them to realize that some things can be understood if

you simply look and think, that others can be figured out with someone else's help, and that searching for information adds more to the "knowing," yet some subjects remain mysteries even to experts. In fact, it's the questions that come up that drive them to further exploration and the accumulation of new knowledge—as we will see in the next example.

VTS AND SCIENCE: AN EXAMPLE

Science is a subject dear to the heart of Craig Madison, who had a twenty-year career as an architect before—inspired by watching his own daughter learn—he decided to become a teacher fifteen years ago. He has spent his second life at the K–5 El Verano Elementary School in Sonoma, California, where after a few years teaching second grade, he switched to third, where he has happily remained. Craig's students match the school's overall population: roughly 80 percent Hispanic, 70 percent ELLs, 85 percent free or reduced lunch. While the school's scores aren't great, they tell little about the kind of education that's going on at El Verano, led by an inspiring principal, Maite Iturri, and dedicated, talented teachers.

VTS has been used schoolwide since the 2007–2008 school year. Working with some university-based consultants, the faculty is operating as inventively as a team as Brian did by himself. It is in the process of developing what it calls an "indigenously designed" curriculum to make language learning central to all lessons, not simply a subject taught in isolation. Part of the school's inspiration was seeing students discussing works of art, putting language into action. The staff decided to make discussion a part of other lessons, and they are designing these themselves "indigenously."

The following is a description of student conversations arising from a combination of hands-on, inquiry-based science and VTS questioning strategies, sent to me by Craig. The science being taught is about the phenomenon of shadows, and Craig gets the ball rolling with a straightforward VTS discussion of an image of a large wall, blank except for the silhouettes of a tree, a bench, and the well-defined shadows of two women, apparently in animated conversation.

Inquiries like this are part of El Verano's indigenously designed English Language Development (ELD) curriculum, which uses science as a vehicle. Our primary goals for Science/ELD have been to develop language through conversation, and a communal construction of meaning through shared observation and evidence.

During a lesson on indoor shadows, I used the standard VTS opening prompt. I asked students to take a moment to find an interesting indoor shadow and to look at it carefully. Students are very familiar with this request because of our schoolwide VTS adoption and the ubiquitous use of VTS questioning strategies, which integrate so well with inquiry. The students were then asked: "So, what is going on here?"

Alfredo and Jason showed me a shadow on a desk and said they weren't sure if the image they were seeing was a shadow or a reflection of the hand held above the desk surface. At this point, I paraphrased their comments about the phenomenon. Jason asked the question: "Can a shadow be a reflection too?" to which I replied, "Could you design an investigation to find out?"

Sam and Maria showed me a shadow on the floor of a pencil with a brightly colored barrel. They pointed out that the shadow was not grey or black, but the bright color of the pencil. Maria said the pencil seemed to be blocking light and reflecting light so it was both a shadow and a reflection. I said, "Maria thinks this shadow might be an example of what Jason asked about . . . a shadow that is a reflection too. She said she thinks so because she can see the color of the pencil in the shadow on the floor."

Aaron and Jeremy said that another object was making three shadows. When I asked what they'd seen that made them say that, they showed me the overlapping, multidirectional shadows of a chair on the floor. I asked them what could make three shadows and they said there must be three light sources, unless one light source could make three shadows. Aaron explained that if you shine light on one side of an object, then a shadow appears on the opposite side. I asked where the light sources might be coming from to make the three shadows, and the boys began looking for light coming from opposite the shadow directions. Jeremy said some light was coming from the window to the north, while Aaron said some light was coming from the fluorescent fixture above. Alvaro, who had been listening to the conversation, said the high windows on the south wall were making more light and might be responsible for the third shadow.

In all these discoveries, VTS encouraged students to look further, listen in, look for their own examples, and share their explanations. I was amazed by how this simple activity engaged the students thoroughly and for an extended amount of time. It was as if they had never had the permission to look carefully and long at the simple shadows around them . . . or that perhaps they had not before had a method to process or make sense of what they were seeing. The use of VTS in art images and in looking at text had apparently developed in these students sensitivity to and appreciation of subtleties that may have gone unnoticed in the past.

The following conversation came about as my students practiced poster presentations of their self-designed investigations. As students acted out their presentations in front of our class before taking them "on the road"—[to present to the other third grade]—their peers offered compliments on their work, made suggestions to make them stronger, and asked for clarifications.

In one instance, Maria showed how her team had tried to cast a shadow on ice, but had found none. This brought a disagreement from another team, who asked for proof of this. Maria showed how the shadow of her hand made a clear shadow in areas around the ice but not on the ice. But the other team said they saw a shadow . . . that the ice was darker when the hand blocked the light . . . that even though the shadow did not have sharp edges, it was still a shadow. The class concurred with this and Maria's team honestly admitted that they saw the shadow cast.

I asked if they wished to revise their claim and they said they did. "But what should we say to the other class about our poster? It has something we don't think is true now." It was such a perfect opportunity to explain to Maria that she and her group were brilliant scientists who thought one idea was true, but changed their minds when they had new information. This was something they could share with other students to show them how to move from an old idea to a better one.

All along the way, when students have questions—Do clouds cast shadows? Does glass? Will an airplane make a shadow on the ground? On a cloud? On a tree? On water?—they are recorded on posters displayed in the classroom. Craig takes the time to search for images that he projects without explanation to give the students a chance to see and talk about the phenomenon that interested them, supporting their self-generated curiosity. Students make often-playful shadow photographs of their own. Craig also searches the VTS-supplied images and other art to find ones with shadows. He inserts these from time to time into VTS discussions to see if the learning carries over from the science lessons to a different context. Reflecting on all of this, Craig adds:

I have noticed that VTS creates the best conditions for learning during science inquiry. One condition is the allowance of adequate time. As opposed to packaged, scripted curricula that seem analogous to a train that leaves the station with the students on it or not, VTS helps teachers break out of pacing constraints and to adapt to the emergent wonderings of students. Giving students adequate time to observe, ponder, and discuss allows deeper patterns and themes to emerge.

Another dramatic premise that VTS dismisses from most inquiry-learning environments is the "predetermined answer." VTS invites students to the table to discover new information, new ways of seeing, and new interpretations of what has been seen before. This shift of attention away from the teacher as the authority dispensing knowledge allows students to construct meaning with personal conviction as they follow where their curiosity leads. They are not merely grasping to find a fixed answer held by the authority. Instead they are actively participating with others in making sense of shared experiences, and are contributing to authentic conversations where the direction of inquiry is affected by what they think and say and do.

VTS AND LANGUAGE: SOME EXAMPLES

Carol Henderson has found another way to make a school assignment mean something in real-world terms. Carol is an artist who makes good use of school holidays to keep her practice going, but she's always been interested in teaching as well. She was an art specialist in the Old Adobe school district back in the day when such existed. Old Adobe is a four-school district within the city limits of Petaluma, California, a city of just under sixty thousand people in mostly-rural Sonoma County, not far from El Verano. The city developed in part because of ranching in the area, and was once known as the "Egg Capital of the World." Today, the city's population is diverse; it benefits from being close enough to San Francisco for some to commute to homes there, but far enough that not all that many do. It feels like a small town. To maintain her commitment to teaching, Carol has taken a variety of grade-level positions within the district when vacancies occurred, most of them temporary. She learned of VTS while taking a summer workshop at the Oakland Museum on a hunch that it might be interesting.

Carol was attracted partly because VTS integrates art into classrooms despite the absence of specialist art teachers, and also because it shows others that art can be useful in ways most don't suspect. She returned to school with the intent to bring VTS to the attention of other teachers and administrators, and she did a painstaking job of letting others in on her discovery. During that period, she taught a variety of

grades at the Old Adobe School, where her principal, Jeff Williamson—
who makes it a practice to pay attention to what interests his teachers—
became intrigued. So did another teacher, our friend Tracy McClure,
who was initially skeptical and in part won over by Carol's enthusiasm.
The two of them were the first to implement; the entire faculty—some
with great enthusiasm, some with less—now includes VTS in the curriculum at all grades.

When the position she had at Old Adobe was filled by a teacher returning from leave, Carol moved to Miwok Valley Elementary School,
taking VTS with her. Because of the struggle the school has with
scores, the climate wasn't right for implementing it across the grades,
but her new principal, Kim Harper, was delighted to have someone in
the school with expertise and interest. Carol found herself faced with
a sixth-grade class of disengaged students when she started. Miwok's
students reflect the lower end of the economic spectrum in Petaluma,
and slightly more than half are Latino, more than half are economically
disadvantaged, and virtually half are ELLs; 17 percent have some form
of disability. The school's scores hover around 50 percent proficiency
in language, math, and science, making it the Old Adobe district's most
challenged school.

Carol felt her sixth graders needed the boost that VTS could give
them, and she began with the art provided by VTS. When she saw how
the students responded to image discussions, she expanded the program, instituting an "image a day" policy, usually starting the day with
a discussion of an image she pulled from a multitude of sources including the day's news and pop culture. She enumerated her goals this way:
she wanted to engage the students in learning, validate their interests
and backgrounds, increase observational skills, develop vocabulary
while they practice oral language and complex syntax, expose them to
"other realities," develop empathy, and let them have a chance to search
for coherence in a fragmented world.

This served her particularly well when her students were struggling
over the curricular necessity of learning to write letters in language

arts. She decided to give the assignment some spice by suggesting the students address their letters to U.S. soldiers on active duty during the war in Afghanistan. The results of their letters were still lackluster, however, and from reading them, she determined that the kids didn't really know much, if anything, about the war or the country. Carol's remedy was to select images that would inform them about the place, the conflict, and what it was like to be fighting in it.

She found a one-page information poster produced by the New America Foundation, a Washington-based think tank, that looks like a page from a contemporary encyclopedia and contains a digest of information, including statistics about the U.S. war effort and details about military operations, ethnic rivalries, the drivers of the Afghan economy, the role of Pakistan, maps, and more.[3] It's a dense compendium of information but as readable as a popular news magazine might make it. She also found a satellite photo of the region with its combination of mountains and dry flatlands, with the boundary of the country outlined above the topography; it has no caption or other explanatory text. She presented another image, also without captions, of a long line of men carrying heavy building supplies up a mountain trail and a picture of a wide-open highway taken from within a military vehicle—we can see the driver's helmet in silhouette, against a stretch of highway heading straight through a wide valley. In the distance is another military jeep, an oncoming motorcycle, and a white-robed Afghani walking alongside the pavement.

As they examined all this material over several days, students talked themselves into ideas, topics, and questions that gave the new drafts of their letters an authenticity that had been lacking before they had a picture of what "our soldiers fighting in Afghanistan" actually meant. The students could now see why letters from home might be meaningful.

In general, what was gained from an image a day? Carol listed what she observed: student engagement, keener observations, thoughts about where the photographer might be and how the shot was captured (a line of inquiry useful when she asks them to think about an author's point of view), and questions about where the photos are from and if additional information was provided in the form of captions, for example. She also valued more specific contributions to the discussions:

> *I remember a day when we were having a discussion about a picture that involved women wearing headscarves, and one second language student turned to an English native and asked what the name of the piece of cloth was that was covering the woman's head. The word* veil *was nonchalantly supplied by the other student, providing the first student with a more precise word for his comment. Rather than completing a vocabulary exercise designed by me, the students ably helped each other gain specificity. The word* veil *continued to come up numerous times throughout the year in many different contexts, but no support was needed due to its organic insertion into the vernacular.*

Debra Vigna offers another slant on this. Cited earlier, Deb teaches second grade at Laurelhurst School in Portland, Oregon, a K–8 school described by the city's newspaper as "outstanding" across the board. Also according to the paper, it has almost no minority students, 1 percent are ELL, and 15 percent qualify for free or reduced lunch. Between 2006 and 2011, the average of students in all grades exceeding proficiency on reading, writing, math, and science tests was 87 percent. Its building reminds me of the school I attended: it's gracious and spacious, though much remodeled and contemporary in the resources it contains. It seems to represent the kind of school in which most of us wouldn't mind picturing ourselves as either students or teachers.

Deb uses linking in a way that reveals her four-year experience with VTS. She's a master of facilitation, and in addition to linking related comments, she often identifies the kind of thought she hears from students, and has noted its effect. For example, she will introduce a paraphrase with the observation, "You were just summarizing what you've been hearing." As she paraphrases the child's thought, and adds the vocabulary describing the kind of thought, she creates a context for several things at once: she validates the comment (and thus the student), she introduces a new vocabulary word in context, and she introduces the possibility of second graders becoming aware of their own thinking—exactly what Marion Bageant suspects is happening with hers in Spokane. Once Deb has folded words like *summarizing* into a paraphrase, the kids repeat the word subsequently; the vocabulary word is used appropriately. Many teachers have heard phrases such as "I concur" coming from students. In the next chapter, you'll see writing samples that include language similarly picked up from paraphrases.

Part of Carol Henderson's inspiration for an "image a day" was her colleague Tracy McClure's "poem a day" conversations with her sixth graders at the Old Adobe School. Old Adobe has different demographics from Miwok. Only a quarter of its student body is classified as economically disadvantaged and it has about half as many English learners; less than 10 percent of the students have disabilities. While Miwok's scores are around 50 percent, Old Adobe students do better on tests; in 2009–2010 their scores averaged 68 percent proficient in language arts, 71 percent in math, and 84 percent in science. Tracy's class scored 87 percent proficient in 2012.

In the lesson plans provided by VTS, we suggest teachers apply the familiar method to poems and short stories, because literature is similarly open to interpretation and requires a focused attention for its deeper meanings to emerge. That said, anything that requires reading is off-putting to those who lack confidence in their reading ability, and that group is not limited to officially classified ELLs. We were therefore half-hearted about recommending the practice. The level playing field might not remain quite so level. Our fears have proved wrong, as Tracy's example—admittedly pretty ambitious in its everyday nature—shows.

Tracy had incorporated poetry into her sixth-grade language arts lessons for years, convinced in part that if students were expected to become good writers, they needed many models to help them understand what that means. And they needed to experience writing in a way that helped them feel the power of words, the effects of considered expression, the breadth of available words, the rich potential in thought-ful use of language. She included poems as part of students' preparation for writing assignments, therefore, and for the most part dissected po-ems for the students, some of whom felt, like perhaps some grownups do, that poetry was a groaner. But Tracy stuck to her guns, and she and others saw positive results even before the advent of today's crop of tests. Her kids went on to middle schools, regarded as good writers.

That didn't stop Tracy from wondering if the teaching couldn't be made better. Once she saw VTS in operation with visual arts, she thought, "Aha! Here's a way to make my approach consistent and to give the kids a more active role!" After a year of using VTS with images, she applied the technique to discussions of poetry to see if kids arrived at the appreciation of language she sought, ideally one that might impact their writing. She rephrased the questions slightly to accommodate the fact that kids were examining writing instead of images, just as Brian did. For the second question, she uses "What did you read that makes you think that?" Or even "What line?" or "What word made you think that?" to help home in on specifics. Over time, even the recalcitrant became as engaged as she hoped.

Tracy isn't sparing with her choice of poems. She was inspired by former poet laureate Billy Collins's Poetry 180 project, sponsored by the Library of Congress.[4] Collins compiled an anthology of poems, one for each school day, geared toward high school. The poems are by contem-porary poets, and are selected in the way we choose images for VTS: the words are usually familiar, but how the words are put together and what they add up to is unpredictable and makes you think. Tracy's choices are at least as adventurous as those of Collins, as you will learn from reading the following comment, sent to me in a welcome e-mail, about what she feels as a teacher:

> *I have to say that there are many things that make my teacher's heart sing, and doing these VTS poetry discussions often leads to such feelings. My students are doing some amazing work with Poe's "The Raven" but*

two days ago, we discussed one by Emily Dickinson, "As Imperceptibly as Grief," which has lots of antiquated language. One student wanted to know the meaning of perfidy, *and no one in the group could answer, so immediately ten or fifteen kids whipped out dictionaries to look it up, and at least that many recorded the meaning on their copies of the poem. Then, as we continued to discuss the poem, I noticed seven or eight kids furtively thumbing through their dictionaries, apparently looking up other challenging words. When I noticed them trying to "sneak" research, I said that it would be fine for them to look up other words and bring the definitions to the group's attention. Oh, my goodness! Students with such a desire to make meaning of text that they refuse to have that information withheld and go to the dictionary for help without being directed to do so. Miracles do happen.*

Old Adobe principal Jeff Williamson, a constant and astutely critical observer of what happens in the classrooms of his school, has written to me that because of experiences like this, "Our students devour literature." Perhaps underlining that point, during one parent/student/teacher conference, a student complained to Tracy, "I used to be a fast reader, but you've ruined me. Now I have to stop and think about what I'm reading." Her mom didn't seem to see this as a problem.

Despite the occasional complaint, the effects of these daily excursions into poetry aren't lost on the students themselves; here's a reflection by one of Tracy's sixth graders:

When you discuss a poem, everybody gets a different picture in his or her head. When you are discussing art, the picture is just in front of you, and there aren't any different pictures in your head, just the one you see. But in poetry, you get different images in your head that describe your interpretation of the poem, and every person's image could be slightly different. With poetry you can imagine anything you want the poem to be as long as there is evidence in the poem to support your idea. Every time someone else shares their ideas, you get more pictures in your head that illustrate what others have described, so you end up with many different pictures for a single poem. It's like every person has a different movie in his head, so at the end you get to have lots of different movies for everything you read and discuss.

Perhaps more telling, Tracy recently received the following unsolicited note from a "high-achieving, all-around wonderful student who was in my class the first year I tried VTS with poetry. She is a tenth grader now. It is nice to know that she sees the connection between our poetry discussions and textual analysis."

Every morning, we did Poem of the Day, and I always wondered why we needed to do that, but now I see how much it has helped. Now, in English, I get excited when we get into poetry because we did so much of it, it's easier for me to understand how to analyze pieces of literature.

IN SUMMARY

To restate for the sake of emphasis, these later applications of VTS wouldn't work without the prior experience both teachers and students have with discussions of art. The fact that art is visual, not text-based; that it is accessible and still puzzling; that it is open to interpretation; that it deals with subjects of wide appeal; that it is varied and complex; that it plays with both ideas and emotions: all these elements, unique to art, are key to making VTS as a discussion strategy applicable to other topics.

As we have seen, it's a very short leap to apply VTS to discuss certain kinds of texts, especially poetry; since VTS focuses on meaning making in art, it feels natural to discuss meanings in literature in the familiar open-ended way. But as we've also seen, teachers also apply it to introduce vocabulary and math problems that little else in students' experience sets them up to understand. Many use it in social studies and science in different ways, but in each case address the shared objectives of trying to engage all students in the active processes required to understand something, particularly to take on unfamiliar material and to dig into it with depth and authentic insight.

We see in the examples given here that a variety of subjects and topics can be covered. I have, logically, included ones that illustrate the phenomenon well, but I have many on file and have only to ask once for teachers to willingly recall and recount their experience. As with virtually all of the steps along the way of creating VTS and learning from the process, teachers have been our mentors and guides. At first we thought that VTS could be applied only to art. It began to dawn on us that material similar to art—open to interpretation—could provoke good discussions and productive learning. Teachers, however, showed us that the field of what is discussable is wider than we thought, perhaps because even if certain, say, scientific explorations end up seeking "right" answers, the way to get to the answers is open-ended. Many, perhaps most, math problems have more than one way of being understood and solved. Scientists and historians look at their data from more vantage points than getting to a specific truth; they need to probe for details, discrepancies, outliers, and additional examples not only to support whatever thesis they develop but also to stay alert to the questions that come up as they search, ponder, and wonder. What teachers have discovered is that VTS discussions mirror an essential process in making discoveries of all sorts.

Little by little, students talk themselves into understanding bits and pieces of the world we live in as well as the material we want them to learn. They learn how to learn, how to think, and how to communicate effectively with others. They use expressive experience with words to aid them in writing. Writing is not so much taught as learned, included in school as it is in life, as a useful tool for recording what one thinks and wants to communicate to others. It's authentic.

CHAPTER 4

Assessing Thinking Through Writing

ASKED TO WRITE ABOUT what he thought was going on in a Winslow Homer painting called *Snap the Whip* (see figure 4.1)[1] on a November day, a third grader responded:

> *I see that those people are pulling on each other. Or trying to catch someone.*

The following May, after ten VTS lessons spread throughout the year, he was asked to write about the same picture, and he had this to say:

> *I think the boys are farmers that are playing a game. I think they are farmers because they are all wearing farmer hats. And I think maybe they are in school because I see the red thing behind the boys that looks like a small school. And I see that some of the boys do not have shoes. I think their family does not have that much money.*

It's not so hard to see differences between the two, and I suspect they make most of us smile. The second is longer, for example, but more importantly, the student provides more (and more detailed) observations, draws more inferences, and gives evidence to support those inferences—significant changes.

Figure 4.1

One of VTS's distinguishing characteristics is how it nurtures the thinking we see in evidence here. Given two samples of writing (one before and one after ten VTS lessons), we have a kind of test—even if it doesn't feel like one—that we can use to assess change or growth. As a test, it documents a great deal more than most standardized varieties. The short-answer and multiple-choice tests that have materialized over the past fifteen years are narrow indicators of students' abilities. In contrast, the open-ended format of this assignment gives us data about the child's command of writing rules and vocabulary, how this eight-year-old functions as a thinker, and how he has changed over six months.

Standardized tests are easy to mark; this requires more. Some of it is not hard: virtually all teachers know how to mark for spelling, punctuation, and sentence structure. The challenge is identifying and understanding the student's increasingly complex thinking, the cause of the marked differences between the samples.

In this chapter I describe what we have learned about VTS-nurtured thinking and how to assess it through examining language, especially writing. Because it asks something more of already burdened teachers, I'll discuss this in the context of the current emphasis on another form of testing.

VTS: WHAT DATA SHOWS

Abigail Housen's and my initial ambitions were simply to advance visual literacy (or, more accurately, *aesthetic thought*, in Housen's terms), and our early studies focused on documenting such change. Still, we remained attentive to what teachers told us while implementing the experimental curriculum. By the time we began a five-year research project in Byron, Minnesota, to study growth in aesthetic thought over the years of elementary school as a result of VTS, Housen and her colleague Karin DeSantis had enlarged the scope of their research to see if they could document another phenomenon reported by teachers: the transfer of skills practiced during VTS to other lessons. Did, for example, asking "What did you see that makes you say that?" lead to a habit of providing evidence, and if so, was that habit independently transferred by students to other lessons? Would they offer reasons to back up an opinion when talking about something in science or when talking about a story, too? It was an interesting question to pursue because it rarely happens: learning something in one context and internalizing the behavior in such a way that, without prompting, we apply it in another.

The news from Housen's five years of study in this rural Minnesota community was good. She then repeated the research in another three-year project in a city, and the findings were even more positive: through VTS, students do indeed learn a strategy they can and will employ, without prompting, to make sense of what is unfamiliar both in art and objects of another nature—like fossils or scientific implements—probing what they see for more than first impressions. Housen was able to document a range of cognitive behaviors—within the spectrum known as *critical thinking*—that were reliably transferred after a certain amount of VTS.

But where might this impact be felt in school? Beginning back in the late 1990s, everyone wanted any new teaching intervention to boost achievement on the tests that were being introduced across the nation, and in some of our experiments, VTS did. Test scores went up, and in a couple of instances—Byron being one of them, a Florida study another[2]—they rose significantly. But it didn't happen in others. What we saw instead was that the impact of VTS on scores depended on what was required by the test. VTS nurtures a rich complexity of thought, more complicated than most tests ask for, and it therefore doesn't help much with multiple-choice or right-/wrong-answer questions, or with placing the correct word in the right form in the proper sequence in a sentence.

Where it does help is when students are asked to provide evidence, and a percentage of test questions requires that skill. As more tests begin to reflect the Common Core standards—which seek what some call *higher-level thinking skills*—there will be more correlation between strong test performance and the preparation that VTS provides.

Housen and DeSantis tracked and wrote about two behaviors: what they call *supported observations* (giving evidence to back up observations without a prompt) and *speculation* (considering multiple possibilities). Harvard's Project Zero did a modest study of the first draft of VTS still in use as a school program at MOMA after I left to concentrate on VTS, and found that it produced evidential reasoning, among other behaviors.[3] A separate federally funded, three-year study (conducted in schools participating in a VTS project of the Isabella Stewart Gardner Museum in Boston) found evidence of significant increases in observations and interpretations as well as notable differences between the treatment group (which had VTS) and the controls (which didn't) in the act of supplying evidence.[4]

Here's how we summarize the collective findings of these studies as well as ongoing observations of student behaviors, very much including what we learn from the analysis of writing samples such as the preceding one on *Snap the Whip*:

As a result of VTS, participants make more observations than when they started, and their observations become more complex, including more detail. Single observations come to be seen in a context.

Over time, participants draw more and more complex inferences from what they see, making meaning of their observations. They develop the habit of providing evidence to back up inferences, interpretations, and opinions.

While at first they might be content with a single idea, they come to speculate among possible meanings, often holding several as equally plausible.

After some time, they might counter their own first thoughts and knowingly revise earlier impressions.

They also begin, at some point, to cycle back to earlier ideas to add detail or to clarify.

This is a fairly hefty array of skills to predict in every fifth grader who's had twenty to thirty hours of VTS, beginning in third grade. They illuminate an invaluable but little-acknowledged capacity of art: deep encounters with visual art are useful in teaching people to think. Housen's early work showed how rich thinking about art could be, even at early viewing stages. Her VTS-related research traced how particular thinking behaviors emerge and develop over time given the VTS method of looking at, thinking about, and discussing art. (Abigail Housen is the appropriate source for detailed, peer-reviewed reports of what she determined.[5])

Housen's data showed something else interesting: that the thinking skills observed in the spring of one school year of VTS are still in place after summer vacation, and the arc of growth is continuous over a multiyear period. This shouldn't be surprising, but it seems as if many teachers feel that students return to school in the fall having forgotten most of what they were supposed to learn the year before. Not with VTS.

Paying attention to new discoveries about how the brain functions helps explain why this happens. VTS employs cognitive operations that are basic to human learning. It is an enormously efficient method of teaching because it conforms to the ways our brains operate to understand the world around us.

Before neuroscience had today's tools for studying the brain, the mid-twentieth-century psychologist Rudolf Arnheim[6] argued persuasively that the act of perception could not be usefully separated from cognition: as soon as our sense organs take in information, our brain begins to process it—recognizing and sorting what we see, hear, touch, or taste. We immediately know to be afraid or to laugh, for example. He says, "Perceiving and thinking are indivisibly intertwined."

In the preface of his pioneering 1969 book *Visual Thinking* (after which VTS was named), Arnheim summarizes what he later argues with examples in a lengthy analysis of research:

> *A review of what is known about perception, and especially about sight, made me realize that the remarkable mechanisms by which the senses understand the environment are all but identical with the operations described by the psychology of thinking. Inversely, there was much evidence that truly productive thinking in whatever area of cognition takes place in the realm of imagery.[7]*

Arnheim's view was that our eyes are particularly useful to us, and usually work in tandem with our ears, and this symbiosis helps us learn to talk. We see something, and eventually associate it with a sound—the words spoken to us by a parent, maybe—and over time we develop speech. As excited as we get at baby's first utterances, sharing the news with anyone who will listen, we should probably show even more respect for the competence this early learning demonstrates, how greatly it's informed by what the baby sees, and the discriminating thinking that comes very early. Think what remarkable acuity it takes, for example, to differentiate between a ball and an orange—superficially very similar—and how early this happens. Almost as quickly, still before speech, children can identify pictures of balls and oranges; we count on this to help them learn words and the alphabet.

At this point, scientists are able to actually trace the pathways this process takes as information proceeds from our eyes and ears to the visual cortex (which processes what we see) and/or the auditory cortex (which processes what we hear). As more information accumulates, scientists will be able to tell us more about how information taken in is quickly identified—it happens almost instantaneously—and passes to the language centers where we continue to make sense of it through putting what we see, for example, into words.

The development of various thinking skills happens so naturally within VTS that it seems a no-brainer, but there aren't many other ways out there to nurture thinking and it's virtually impossible to teach in isolation. Like listening, it is hard to teach outside a context. The habit of providing evidence to back up ideas, for example—what's also called *evidential reasoning*—doesn't happen just because any of us wants it to. If it did, we would never need to ask the second VTS question: what do you see that makes you say that? But practice shows us that we do: even in discussion among adults, you'll hear the facilitator repeating the question frequently. Most of us have managed to get to adulthood—with pretty good educations to boot—without the practice becoming habitual. We state what we think without saying why. Look at news media: we don't need to look very critically to see how rarely commentators provide evidence to back up their assertions about a huge range of topics.

Reasoning becomes a relevant behavior as an aspect of the learner knowing she needs to figure something out, wanting to understand it, having the motivation to probe for explanations, and being curious enough to look for reasons. Despite the fact that it's called a higher-level thinking skill, suggesting that it's more an endpoint than a start, humans have the capacity for an early form of reasoning even when tiny. Consider this: "Mommie's smiling," a baby must think, "so everything is okay and I can smile too." Or a bit later: "Daddy's looking unhappy," worries the toddler, "Have I done something wrong?" That's the start of reasoning, trying to figure out what certain observations—such as facial expressions—tell us. The desire to understand is also the behavior behind the question "Why?" asked so often as three- and four-year-olds explore the world. It's why many kids take things apart. But like many other behaviors we see operating in small children, it seems it's an instinct that gets lost along the path of growing up and, perhaps significantly, going to school.

At the moment parents and teachers want to teach a behavior like reasoning and to try to foster it as a habit, we have to simulate a circumstance as authentic as a little one trying to read the meaning of expressions. Most productively, we create an environment that incorporates motivation, opportunity, and the appropriate assists that cognitive scientist Lev Vygotsky recommends—staying developmentally appropriate. We seek the form of reasoning children can do.

We did not know searching for meaning in art could be such a context until we watched it happen and then tracked it. We predicted that the second VTS question—the one seeking evidence—was within the cognitive reach of beginning viewers, but we didn't know that it would become internalized and then applied in other contexts until Abigail Housen and Karin DeSantis completed their studies. We didn't know that the social dynamics created by VTS facilitation would allow the thinking of classmates—revealed in comments—to assist the thinking of others, an example of "the more capable peer"[8] providing a rung (i.e., an observation or idea) on which another can climb.

We ask a question that is worded to make it easy for the responder to supply evidence, drawing on the familiar practice of thinking: the eye/mind connection. "What do you see," we ask, "that makes you say that?" Students don't have to pull an answer from memory. Nor do they have to have to examine their motives, as "Why do you think that?" would frame the activity. They just identify the observations on which they've based an inference.

One reason this is easy to do is that, according to Housen, beginning viewers tend to see things concretely: "It's a girl," they will say, looking at a particular figure in a picture. This jibes with Jean Piaget's analysis of children's cognition during these years: whatever they think is most likely related directly to concrete observations and the appearance of things. If questioned, they would know it was actually a *picture* of a girl, but that's not how they see it when they are looking on their own. That makes it easy to answer the question, "What do you see that makes you say it's a girl?" "She has long hair." Meanwhile, another beginning viewer might think it was a boy, based on what he sees: the figure is holding a ball, which signals "boy" to him. Neither is likely to consider two possibilities, at least not for a while, such as it could be either; boys can wear their hair long and girls also play with balls. They come to do so over time and repeated opportunity to hear and discuss options with their peers.

And, of course, we can't expect either to think the girl is a symbol of, say, innocence. When they infer something from the image—for example, "the girl is happy"—it's because they see something concrete (a smile). It's not a mysterious matter. When the question is phrased as it is in VTS, students can supply evidence because it asks them "what they see" that informs their thinking.

Very young children can be stumped by the question, of course, but we've seen four- and five-year-olds answer it in due course, and from ages six or seven on, it seems as if it's fun. Most have made a habit of it by the end of the second or third year of VTS. Talking about her sixth graders in Spokane, Rachel Zender sees it happening in the context of VTS image lessons—she notes when and for whom she no longer needs to supply the second question as a prompt—before she expects it in other classes. As they become accustomed to VTS, however, students want her to stick to the rules of the game: they will alert her if she forgets to ask for evidence, for example. They enjoy the challenge. "But by the end of their second year of VTS," Rachel explains, "I no longer need to ask the questions much of the time." That said, the wording of the question—"What do you see that makes you say that?"—gives her a natural pattern for asking the question in other subjects, and she especially applies it to text, noting that "VTS experience turns the kids' answers from vague to pinpointed."

As listed earlier, providing evidence is only one of the thinking behaviors we've documented, either because of research studies or because of the piling up of anecdotal evidence. Speculation is another, as we saw in writing samples: it *might* be this, or *maybe* it's that. Or elaboration: returning to an earlier comment to add detail. Or revision: *at first* I thought, but *then* I thought. Linda Sugano, another Spokane teacher, talked about how such changes of mind are not easy for fourth graders; they prefer to add or take away, but not to change. She's seen VTS help them go beyond what she's come to expect. One child who was on a "behavioral plan" (his father too) had an issue with having to be right. She told me that she saw him "even becoming able to hold more than one idea in his head at a time. 'I respectfully disagree with myself,' he said at one point in a discussion. Definitely a marked change."

All of this happens because of three things: art, developmentally appropriate assists in the form of a few questions, and the group process enabled by paraphrasing and linking. A particular aspect of paraphrasing assists with developing speculative thinking: rephrasing comments with conditional language, suggesting that an interpretation is a possibility rather than a fact.

One of the prime motivators for schools that implement VTS is to get kids thinking. And one of the main reasons we created so modest an intervention timewise was because we can accomplish our goals in that amount of time. And, as rare as it is, data says that for *all* kids, not just the normally able, the aforementioned thinking behaviors happen within about thirty hours of instruction spread over several years of elementary school.

TRACKING CHANGES IN THINKING THROUGH WRITING

Being able to assess our own growth is a necessary part of becoming functional adults. Successful people know how to understand what they've done, to continue what works, and to fix what doesn't in all sorts of arenas. While self-assessment might happen naturally in some people, most of us have to learn how to be constructively self-critical. In the same way that part of our responsibility as teachers is to make sure our students learn how to learn, we should probably see it as necessary to teach our students how to reflect on what they know and what they don't, and to know what they can do to learn more. We need to do more than grade them, in other words, teaching them how to evaluate the work they do themselves—and to do so in a way that enables them to change what they want to improve. While it seems to be every politician's question, students themselves are the ones who really need to know how they are doing and how to grow.

Standardized testing doesn't necessarily help. Such tests show what the student can recall, under pressure, of material it was usually not her choice to learn. Somebody decides she needs to know algebra and nouns, for example, and whether or not she's actually interested, she sits at her desks and is "taught" so that she "learns." Then she's tested to prove she knows it. Former President George W. Bush voiced his belief in this relationship, saying, "You teach a child to read, and he or her will be able to pass a literacy test." Such tests are scored by someone else, and the results—what she got right or wrong, what she did well or poorly—are perhaps never seen or understood by her at all.

There are reasonable arguments for this process, especially since it works for many kids. But the joy of learning may well be the victim of rote activity in a subject of no personal relevance to the learner, and the significance of any achievement is dubious if it doesn't stick. As a result of a similar instruction and testing, I aced algebra and remember none of it now, and haven't for decades. How about you?

The emphasis on testing we live with today hits hardest those already at risk of not succeeding. The "high-stakes tests" that dominate the school year are unforgiving delineators, and can be destructive to the confidence of the young people found not proficient. What useful purpose is served by saying to the struggling child that he is not as good as others? At some point in life, yes, one has to be equal among competitors; we want all those awarded MDs to have equal levels of core skills and knowledge. But throughout most schooling prior to college, nurturing confidence and a concept of "I can do it" is vastly more important. Otherwise, it's like saying everyone should be 5'10" and if you're either taller or shorter, you get a lousy score. We should expect students of differing capabilities and backgrounds to perform differently, and though the struggling student might achieve less during any given period, we want to ensure he stands a chance of catching up. And he won't if he sees himself as a failure.

All that said, we live in a world where the achievement of students, the effectiveness of teachers, and this form of testing are interlocked. It is likely to remain so for a while; many with authority are committed to it and have invested hugely in it. But many of us are old enough to remember when other grading systems were in play, and it is my view that the pendulum, inevitably, swings. Also in my opinion, we could collectively push the pendulum in a new direction, at least a little, by demonstrating other ways to show students' accomplishments and capabilities: solid, rigorous representations of how students can perform when they are at their best and most holistic—measures that are fair to all students. The advent of Common Core standards sets a framework for such assessment, and I will cycle back to that particular issue later.

One thing that affects performance, and I sometimes feel it's the proverbial elephant no one mentions, is the issue of motivation. We probably learn most easily those things we want to learn; we see them as interesting and useful. The opposite might also be true: it's hard to invest seriously in things we don't see as related to our own needs or curiosity. Similarly, if we are to be successful at helping students become committed to monitoring their growth, any process should connect to their sense of themselves, accurately reflecting both what they know and care about already and where they get; it should be, like all meaningful instruction, student-centered and individualized. Ideally, young people will, as a result, develop a continuous and reflexive behavior of self-assessment over the course of schooling along with the other skills society deems necessary.

Young people, of course, don't know what they need to know. Nor are they aware of all there is to know. Nor are they likely to come up with testing regimens on their own. To some extent, therefore, all curricula introduce unfamiliar material and stress skills not yet exercised by students. If we hope to make them take long and productive looks at their performance, however, we are wiser to align what we teach to their interests, make it reflect what they are ready to know and do, and confine our testing to what they have realistically been able to accommodate.

It is sometimes hard to see that standards writers, curriculum designers, and test creators keep this in mind. Standards came into being in recent decades because it was observed that certain students succeeded in school when others didn't, and those rightfully distressed about this found a remedy they thought would work: hold all schools accountable for meeting certain standards. Dutifully, governments and administrators developed standards in many subjects in state after state, and in some localities. Curriculum materials followed.

The motives for this are unassailable, but the impact has not been what people hoped. Too many teachers can't get through all the material they're supposed to. Too many students leave school with fewer skills than expected, and others still fail to achieve at the level we all desire. Too many students find nothing compelling in school at all and drop out. Meanwhile, the overall curriculum has narrowed to the point where essential subjects are given very short shrift while teachers and students spend most of the time on a few skills that, examined from the distance at which I sit, leave students unprepared in whole arenas of human activity: science, social studies, and—dare I say it?—the arts. And still, levels of proficiency in language and math elude too large a percentage of students.

From the examples of teaching I included in chapter 3, I'm sure you've figured out that I enjoy seeing teachers find inventive ways to approach existing curricula and standards, and also appreciate those who experiment, having decided that the ways given to them fail to engage students as they'd like and still fall short of producing the command of information or skills sought. I'm much encouraged by the progress shown on a standardized test that Marion Bageant's students made with a new approach to exactly what she's supposed to teach. And I also love the notion, introduced in the chapter 3 by Craig Madison, that school faculties can together create "indigenously designed curricula" at El Verano School. Faced with huge issues with a population of ELLs, Principal Maite Iturri and her staff invent ways to build language development into every subject, not just during the language arts block. This not only makes for an authentic approach to language—using it all the time in every pursuit to communicate—but also gives them time to deeply engage students with subject matter that in too many schools gets short-changed, such as science.

But a different kind of teaching merits, perhaps demands, other approaches to knowing what students retain. It's entirely possible to devise fair and helpful tests to show what competencies are in place at the start of any process (necessary as benchmarks), to determine what's missing, and to examine what sticks from lessons taught: what remains useful to students. Each September, let's say, all students could be given a set of tasks that allow them to safely and honestly represent what they know and can do in a variety of arenas. A similar set of tasks, perhaps the same ones, could be given months later to show what's been accomplished, post–instructional interventions. In both cases, the tests should reflect the teaching itself: we should test what is possible to learn given the teaching. The tests should accommodate an uneven playing field, in the way that Marion Bageant made a way for her severely disabled child to make use of a scribe.

Determining achievement should be only one intention of testing. It also has to help the student understand himself and what he can do to grow, and the teacher to know how to guide that growth. Together, both teacher and student should study the results of any assessment, and occasionally parents should take a close look as well.

I don't know how the students studying shadows in Craig's classroom might do on a short-answer test on the phenomenon. But I think they could show what they retained if they were to look at a series of photographs of shadows and explain what they see. At El Verano, two parallel objectives are pursued: the accumulation of knowledge based on curiosity, and the development of adequate language for students to express themselves clearly in all subjects. The achievement of these objectives isn't going to be found in short-answer tests.

In order to advance both the language and scientific goals of the shadow lesson, Craig assigned the task of preparing poster presentations so that students could explain the findings of their small-group, self-designed experiments; we got a taste of that process when he described one group figuring out that an assumption they'd made—that shadows didn't appear on ice—was actually untrue, an assertion called into question by a skeptical classmate. Craig can keep the poster presentations as evidence of their experiments and conclusions as a measure of their accomplishments, augmented by keeping notes on students' verbal exchanges.

I asked Craig to explain more of how he and his fellow teachers assess the learning, and here's his response:

We are interested in finding out where the kids are at the start of a unit, so we open with a discussion, as we did, for example, prior to our Reflected Light inquiry. Usually students meet in a circle and the teacher asks a question: What do we know about reflected light (or rockets, or shadows, or snails, or colored light, or balance, etc.)? This time I used a painting of a reflection as an opener: "No, I think it's water." "It's someone at the beach and the water is reflecting them." Etc. This was, of course, facilitated with paraphrasing and VTS questioning asking for evidence. This part was short—5–10 minutes. Then I asked, "What else do we know about reflected light?" The student comments were recorded on chart paper, which becomes a publicly posted, living document: students added to the poster over time.

As they experiment with materials, they discover more and they are asked to add observations to the chart. The inquiry usually goes on for 12–15 days. Kids may add ideas with Post-it notes or bring them up during Science Talk [which] happens after each day of investigation [and] during which we discuss what we did that day. Part of our intention with these is to encourage the gradual shift from kids relying on the teacher, as the discussion gatekeeper, to kids having a "dinnertime" type of discussion, where they wait for an appropriate pause before interjecting their comments, and address each other rather than speaking always to the teacher. This is important for when they work in small groups, and at the beginning at least, I notice the teacher must moderate the discussion for inclusivity. The talks are usually hybrids of the hand-raising method mixed with "dinnertime." The central VTS ideas of a safe environment to speak, providing evidence, teacher paraphrasing/theme linkage, and civil discussion remain paramount.

An additional chart is generated at the same time as the one that lists "what we know." This has to do with questions that arise as the discussion unfolds. And questions go hand in hand with discussion and observation. The more kids discuss what they think they know about a phenomenon, the more questions arise. The questions are simple at first (Can you see a shadow at night?) and gradually grow more complex as the students are allowed the time to think deeper into the subject. (If we shined 26 lights on one object, how many different types of shadows could we make? Can you make a shadow in shade? Can you make a shadow appear on the same side of an object as the light source that caused the shadow?) All of these questions lead to experimentation either by all of us together or by smaller groups.

We assess in part by comparing the information recorded on posters at the start (written in one color) with the later recordings. At the end of each inquiry, we ask the students an open-ended question, "Now that we have looked carefully at reflected light, let's share what we have learned about it. Tell what you know about reflected light using words and pictures." We don't want a scripted response. By seeing what a student offers—it could be a labeled or unlabeled drawing, a chart, a life-cycle graphic; we also look at the content and quality of their written expression—they reveal their thinking as well as what they know. When we collect more than one such sample, we can compare early inquiry notations with those done later to follow individual student progress.

The analysis tracks movement from simple observations to observations with detail; inferences with and without evidence; hypotheses; and revision of thinking. We keep a tally sheet. This whole process is still in development with us but as we work it out, most teachers are avoiding quantification of results. We have no school district requirement regarding science/ELD at the primary level, so we're focusing on an individualized assessment.

This final point is key: Craig and his fellow El Verano teachers feel free to experiment in both the teaching and the assessment of science. It is clearly easier to maneuver in areas where scores aren't the issue.

While this documentation might not withstand scrutiny by those who need quantifiable data to assume achievement, it represents a model that was in place not so long ago: when teachers were trusted to know how students achieved, and defined achievement in relation to where a student started and to the effort required to reach the endpoint.

ASSESSING THINKING IN WRITING

I opened this chapter with a comparison between two writing samples, one before a sequence of VTS lessons, one afterward. In this section I am going to analyze a second set in more detail as another way to assess growth.

I place my emphasis on examining thinking because increasing complexity of thought is what causes the significant changes in writing. Language is often taught word-by-word, rule-by-rule; what we see in the upcoming samples is likely abetted by such direct instruction, but it comes as the result of engaging, thoughtful, extended discussions.

Housen's work regarding thinking showed a way to analyze writing samples. In the late 1970s she recognized that close coding of remarks could be a way to measure changes in thinking. By 1983 she had developed a scoring manual to do this that sorted empirically derived categories into a developmental sequence. The first step in understanding and assessing changes in thinking involves breaking the writing sample into parts that can be examined individually, a task called *parsing* by Housen. The second is classifying each part, referred to as *coding* by Housen and her research colleague Karin DeSantis.

It was quite simple to parse the writing sample that follows. The entirety of a student's pre-test is one sentence. The image he writes about is again Winslow Homer's *Snap the Whip* (pictured at the opening of this chapter):

I think a bunch of guys rough housing with each other.

Each word and phrase in this is part of a single idea. But I see two distinct kinds of thoughts packed into that short, not-quite-complete sentence: an *observation* ("a bunch of guys") and an *inference* ("rough housing"). The student begins with the qualifying "I think," as if the inferred roughhousing might only be his personal opinion of what's going on with the bunch of guys he sees; this foreshadows a third kind of thought, a *speculation*.

As his teacher, I note that the boy is capable of observation and inference, though on a limited basis. I want him to notice more, and for his description to reflect that. I'm glad he is willing to qualify his comment by starting with "I think," but wonder if some more thought might elicit either more detail or a conclusion other than roughhousing, a reference that must be familiar to him but seems a quick take on the activity. I also see that he needs practice in crafting complete sentences; he's left out a verb here.

Still, I wouldn't judge him harshly; it's not atypical writing for an eight-year-old near the beginning of third grade, and this is a child without a lot of resources in his life beyond school. And I should let him know that I appreciate what he did.

His post-test sample, six months later, gives me more to go on and shows changes I'm delighted to see:

> *I think that boys are playing a game. Behind them and on the side there are houses where they probably live. Also behind the houses is a huge mountain. I think this is a scene long ago and that the house behind them is a barn. The boys look like they are coming in from the barn.*

Clearly the boy has more to say. He looked longer and harder and thought more about what he saw, and it shows in his writing. He seems to follow a certain logic, beginning with what he sees as the central action (this time a more accurate assessment of what's happening: a game, not roughhousing), and following up with illustrative details about the setting. At the end, he cycles back to the action, suggesting that the boys might have emerged from a building behind them. Happily, I note that each sentence is complete, a change from his first sample.

Forgive me if I get a bit wonky here. As a teacher interested in understanding the writing and the changes, I want to show how I would isolate sentences and phrases that seem to constitute specific complete thoughts:

> *I think that boys are playing a game.*
> *Behind them and on the side there are houses where they probably live.*
> *Also behind the houses is a huge mountain.*
> *I think this is a scene long ago/*
> *and that the house behind them is a barn.*
> *The boys look like they are coming in from the barn.*

In examining this, I decide that all but one of the sentences is a distinct unit, and each includes detail as well as a central idea. I'm glad to see so many more observations and more detail ("huge mountain") and more pinpointing (several "behind" instances and an "along the side"). While he made just one inference in his pre-test, he makes five here: the references to a game, to where the boys live, to the era, to a barn, and to where the action comes "in from." That represents significant change; he's learned to pull more meaning from the image. The fourth and more complex sentence bridges two ideas: one inference about time ("a scene long ago") and a second referring to the structures behind ("the house . . . is a barn").

I can now identify each type of thought I find—"observations," "detailed observations," and "inferences." I can actually make a comparative count of the two pieces of writing. The student's first contains one simple observation and one inference. His second has one simple observation, two detailed observations, and five inferences. That graphs easily. I can add to it an assessment of spelling and grammar, both excellent.

Interestingly, I note that my student also starts two comments with "I think" and in the second sentence he writes, "where they *probably* live." By doing this, he suggests that his ideas are only possibilities and that others might see things differently; the boys might actually live somewhere else, for example. As noted earlier, Housen refers to this as *speculative thinking* or *speculation*, and thinks of it as one cornerstone of critical thinking: holding a number of ideas as possible at one time. It's the kind of thinking that allows us to deal comfortably with subjects and situations that are not simple or easy to put into cubbyholes—like most of science, much of medicine, and many issues in society. To be able to tackle problems in these arenas, we have to be able to look at them from many sides and consider multiple solutions. This boy shows the dawning of a capacity to think in that complex mode, not certain he's right but nonetheless confident enough to put out options. Not a bad skill for a child of eight.

After making the counts, I reflect further on this child. His first sample contained one somewhat idiosyncratic idea. The second was more grounded and made more sense in terms of the picture. What can I learn from that? For one thing, I should watch to see if he applies this more nuanced thinking in other lessons—for example, seeing what he notices from watching our class aquarium or window garden, what conclusions he draws, and whether or not he speculates among possible conclusions. Piecing it all together, I might wonder if he has the makings of a historian, knowing how to use primary sources to develop an understanding of past time, or a scientist, capable of drawing conclusions from observations but staying open to more considerations over time. I wonder how I can help him see these possibilities.

Even if these two samples provided all I knew about this student, I'd know a lot. Certainly I'd know he's capable of change.

In order to start him thinking about his achievement, during the time I set aside for students to read each day—therefore while his classmates were occupied—I'd meet with him to show him the samples I'd kept in a portfolio of his work. I'd also have a printout of the painting at hand, and before we started we'd take a good look at it. Together, we'd spend a few minutes comparing the two samples, noting what he'd seen and how he'd translated that into writing. (Last week I heard a fourth grader in Carol Henderson's current mixed fourth- and fifth-grade class ask, without prompting, to do just that: compare her post test, which she had just written, to the first; Carol promised to meet with her.) I'd surely point to this student how many more observations he made in the second, pointing each out in both samples. I'd be conscious of wanting him to recognize what an observation is, what it consists of.

Since he's only eight, if I used the word *inference*, I'd make sure that I explained it, pointed to examples, and asked him to explain the term in his own words. I'd then ask him to see if he could find inferences on his own, and help by pointing to any he enumerated and others, in the end, that he didn't.

I'd tell him I admired how he'd really thought about what the picture was telling him, and how he'd used the word *probably* to acknowledge that a comment was just one idea; there could be others. And, of course, I'd comment on his perfect spelling and his use of periods at the end of each sentence, and I'd remark that he'd written one sentence very clearly expressing two ideas.

But we wouldn't stop there. We would also look at the picture together, and I'd ask if there was more he might have seen and mentioned, or if, in thinking about it more, he wanted to change anything he'd said. In this concrete way, I'd introduce the concept of adding, editing, or revising—parts of what any good writer learns to do.

I'd end as I'd begun: thanking him for his good work. Were he a bit older, I'd ask what he thought he wanted to work on, to get better at. But I'd make sure he knew I was impressed with his ability.

Over a semester, I'd meet with each of my young writers several times to review such samples. Of course, I would have regularly asked students to write about all sorts of things we'd discussed in class and would therefore have other samples of writing I'd analyzed.

One of the reasons for selecting this young man as the example here is that I have another sample from him—writing he did after discussing an image with his classmates. In the pre- and post-test samples, we see what he could do when assigned to write about an image he was looking at both times on his own: no VTS questions, no classmate input, no preparation by way of his expressing his ideas in class. The following writing comes from his choice of the image to write about (see figure 4.2),[9] and he wrote it several months after the actual discussion.

> I think that in this picture a pig keeper is letting his pigs eat while other people cut down trees as you can see them doing that in the back of the picture. Also I think that they are working for a landlord because you can see a castle in the back. You can also see a dog which is next to the pig keeper and this dog probably helps him keep the pigs from straying away.

If you'll pardon my getting a little excited, I'll point out that we don't have to dig very far to see many sharp and detailed observations and

Figure 4.2

a fluid compound sentence containing two narratives pulled from this strange image. (By the way, what *is* that pig keeper doing?)

This student has added a new kind of thinking: he adds *evidence* to back up one of his inferences: he writes that, because of the castle, he thinks the depicted people work for someone else.

He maintains his "speculative frame of mind," that remarkable quality of implying, "This is what I think is happening; I'm not completely sure; there are likely other possibilities." To me this behavior isn't wishy-washy. It's *open*. It's a quality I wish for in more public discussions. What if, for example, the Sunday morning television pundits stated their positions as possibilities, not certainties? What if, as a corollary, they actually listened to each other, backed up positions with evidence, and debated ideas instead of pontificating—all things this child already knows how to do?

When my student and I review this among other samples of his writing, we'd do as we did before: look back and forth between the writing and the picture to help see what he described in his writing, and what he might want to add or change.

And we'd look to see if his skill at drawing conclusions from complex observations here carried over to the notes in his science journal about a satellite image of a storm system the class also discussed.

In terms of grammar, I'd introduce the idea of complex sentences, pointing to examples. I'd also ask him to think about whether or not any additional punctuation—perhaps a few commas—might make it easier to understand. I'd ask him about the *which* in the next-to-last sentence. I think we'd use the index in a language textbook to look up the rule about when to use *which* and when to use *that*. I'd ask him to think about which would be correct here.

What do you think? If you were this student, do you think you would learn from this process? Could you see me, the teacher, as someone who wanted to help you, not judge you? Would you think we were making good use of our time?

Trying to move beyond hypotheticals here, I wonder about whether or not this would be possible for you as a teacher. Since collecting the writing, saving it, and analyzing it all take a hunk of the little time you have in your schedule, would you be able to fit this in? (Here's a thought if you have any notion of giving this a try: perhaps you could make a small selection of students who particularly need additional assistance to experiment with and see if you could make it work.) Do you think your teacher colleagues would be interested in hearing about it if you did? Would parents? Would administrators understand and support such an effort? Think about this in terms of meeting Common Core objectives.

I've talked about this approach with teachers during VTS implementations in schools, and gotten some heads nodding, but as far as I know, no one has tried it, so it remains an untested hypothesis. (I'll confer with Carol after she meets with her eager fourth grader to get a reality check from her.) As a concept, it relates to a movement spearheaded by Rick Stiggins and the Assessment Training Institute that is working to shift the emphasis from "assessment *of* learning" to "assessment *for* learning."[10] The Institute's point resonates with the intention behind this form of assessment: assessing more holistically and engaging the student in the process of examining and evaluating her own work so that she learns from the assessment activity itself. But as we think about new, more flexible approaches to assessing achievement, take a look at the criteria for the highest level of writing for students in fourth grade in Florida, where this third-grade student lives; Florida doesn't articulate criteria for third grade. To be awarded six points in fourth grade, the highest score, here's what writing is supposed to reflect:

> The writing is focused on the topic, has a logical organizational pattern (including a beginning, middle, conclusion, and transitional devices), and has ample development of the supporting ideas. The paper demonstrates a sense of completeness or wholeness. The writing demonstrates a mature command

of language including precision in word choice. Subject/verb agreement and verb and noun forms are generally correct. With few exceptions, the sentences are complete, except when fragments are used purposefully. Various sentence structures are used.[11]

How close do the second and third writing samples of my third grader come to the highest levels sought by Florida for students a year older? Pretty close. The writing seems natural and easy, yet it's logical, coherent, and fluent in ways that correspond to what authorities in Florida want to see in students a year later. And, of course, it's not a "paper" with the benefit of editing or rewriting, but rather an extemporaneous snapshot of the student's ability.

The advent of the Common Core standards has opened up the goals of instruction to include skills that VTS nurtures very directly. These standards span language arts, social studies, science, and art, though fewer than one might think in art. (At least two reasons for that irony stand out: most standards relate to making art, not looking at it, and the paucity of art specialists in schools and the minimal amount of time, space, and materials allotted to arts instruction make standards impossible to achieve. Classroom teachers can't be expected to fill in the gap. It is also true, in my personal view, that the arts standards are skewed in order to emphasize skills I'd term more academic than artistic; memorizing the color chart, for example, at ages when creating images and objects is way more the point.)

For the moment, in order to understand what VTS can achieve, let's simply look at three "College and Career Readiness Anchor Standards for Speaking and Listening" identified for K–5 in the CCSI guidelines:

Comprehension and Collaboration

Prepare for and participate effectively in a range of conversations and collaborations with diverse partners, building on others' ideas and expressing their own clearly and persuasively.

Integrate and evaluate information presented in diverse media and formats, including visually, quantitatively, and orally.

Evaluate a speaker's point of view, reasoning, and use of evidence and rhetoric.

Does it make sense that VTS could help meet these standards? The first almost describes a VTS discussion, and VTS, in very few lessons, gives students the necessary experience to decode diverse visual media; and if teachers apply it in other lessons, the students learn to "decode" poems, math word problems, scientific imagery, and even constitutional amendments. Every discussion gives students practice at reasoning, using evidence, and articulating a point of view. While directly addressing these specifically, VTS lays a foundation for many more Common Core–defined standards—for reading, writing, and oral language in most disciplines from language arts to social studies to science.

Let's look at the writing samples analyzed earlier through the lens of Common Core standards for third grade.[12] The instruction for writing about images after discussions can be as simple as, "Write what you think is going on. Don't forget to say what you see that makes you say that." It's a looser assignment than many, with decisions about what to write and how to sequence it determined by the student. Here are some of the Common Core writing outcomes; I've left out ones that were irrelevant, such as "uses appropriate technology."

Here's the sample again:

I think that in this picture a pig keeper is letting his pigs eat while other people cut down trees as you can see them doing that in the back of the picture. Also I think that they are working for a landlord because you can see a castle in the back. You can also see a dog which is next to the pig keeper and this dog probably helps him keep the pigs from straying away.

Look back and forth between the standards listed and the sample. Remember, the assignment wasn't to write an "opinion piece" but a description of what's going on in an image. Still the student creates a viable "topic sentence," supplies a "point of view," "provides reasons," and "develops a topic." While not using the linking words specifically, he writes a coherent statement with logical flow.

Grade 3 students can:

Write opinion pieces on topics or texts, supporting a point of view with reasons.

    a. Introduce the topic or text they are writing about, state an opinion, and create an organizational structure that lists reasons.

    b. Provide reasons that support the opinion.

    c. Use linking words and phrases (e.g., *because, therefore, since, for example*) to connect opinion and reasons.

    d. Provide a concluding statement or section.

Write informative/explanatory texts to examine a topic and convey ideas and information clearly.

    a. Introduce a topic and group related information together; include illustrations when useful to aiding comprehension.

    b. Develop the topic with facts, definitions, and details.

    c. Use linking words and phrases (e.g., *also, another, and, more, but*) to connect ideas within categories of information.

    d. Provide a concluding statement or section.

The standards add these elements describing the role of adults in helping students to perform to the desired level. They seem to argue for the kind of assessment suggested earlier.

With guidance and support from adults, produce writing in which the development and organization are appropriate to task and purpose.

With guidance and support from peers and adults, develop and strengthen writing as needed by planning, revising, and editing.

If I were the adult providing "guidance and support" to help the student "develop and strengthen writing," one thing I'd ask him to think about was what he might do to provide a conclusion, something not really needed in this writing sample but sought in the standards. That said, I'd feel we were making good progress toward meeting the standard we still had a couple of months to reach.

You can see that the people who wrote these standards weren't thinking about responses to images, and probably had in mind more typical language arts writing assignments. But you can also see that on most key points, the writing is on or close to the mark sought by the end of grade three.

IN SUMMARY

If nothing else, we can learn from this that ten hour-long discussions of images can help kids achieve at the levels sought by our current system. Referring to both Marion Bageant's student test performance and the Florida evaluation guidelines, this form of teaching—discussion-based—can assist with attaining high levels of student achievement measured by traditional testing. Although tests to measure performance are yet to be created, we can also see significant progress to achieving Common Core writing outcomes.

Were we to show these samples to a colleague or administrator, we would be smart to explain that the writing is about images, and that direct lines can be drawn from behaviors achieved here and ones sought by various standards. As I said earlier, our third-grade student has been taught a ninety-minute-per-day language arts curriculum every day as well, so the language impact doesn't come from VTS alone. But the most useful part of the comparison between the three samples is how the boy wrote after a discussion, even given a delay of months. What could happen if there were more use of discussion, applied across the curriculum? Marion's math lessons provide some insight. So do Craig

Madison's students' behaviors regarding shadows. Discussion, guided by the right questions, is a powerful and too-little-used tool.

I've taken pains here to justify the outcomes of VTS in terms that speak to those who must live by standardized tests and content standards, including the Common Core standards that will, to some extent, unite schools across the country. But the question that comes up for me, finally, boils down to what we mean when we say "student achievement." Here's a comment to weigh as you think about this: a description of what it's meant to a sixth-grade student, who when asked by Tracy McClure to write down what she thought was important about her experience with VTS, said this:

> I recently went to an art show and at each artist's piece that might have caught my eye, the same questions that we used during VTS in class came to me, such as: take a minute to examine this part in the poem or image, what more can we find, and what do you see in the text or art piece that makes you say that. When these phrases come to mind, it can guide you through the art piece. From corner to corner, figure to figure, and color to color these questions will make this piece "whole." Let's just say, this can really help you find a deeper meaning in an art piece!

I hope you have read between the lines of this chapter: I think the definition of achievement that now measures the effectiveness of teaching and of teachers is too narrow. When I, at least, see Craig's students becoming thoughtful, imaginative, rigorous scientists and Tracy's students learning to "devour literature," I think that the passage of tests tells way too little, and might not even accommodate the kind of accomplishment that will enable the young people in our care to eventually help fix the world, now ailing in so many ways. The child who in sixth-grade knows to look for "deeper meaning"—whether it's in art, clouds, or human behavior—is a child empowered in a way that correct word choice or spelling doesn't begin to describe.

CHAPTER 5

VTS, Language Development, and English Language Learners

AS YOU KNOW, SINCE SHE was a toddler, my ever-present learning lab, Wyla, has continuously had her nose to the ground—or up to the sky—whenever we are outside. Like virtually all kids, she's curious and observant, and her interest in the countless little things she finds often outlasts mine, though one of the magical aspects of grandparenthood is patience lacking when her father was young. As a matter of course, the adults in Wyla's life identify what she notices, and among her first words were names of the things she found fascinating.

Particularly when she was three and four, when we took walks, her intention was rarely arrival at a place, but instead to see what we found along the way—sticks, insects, caterpillars, lizards, flowers, scents, stones, odd formations of whatever. Even at the zoo or natural history museum, it was the little things she noticed outside of cases and pens that grabbed her focus, like balancing on a curb, running up or down a ramp, or playing in the fountain. Sure, she looked at the elephants and giraffes, and knew their names, recognizing them from books and puzzles—she easily named shapes as she moved decals around the ubiquitous sticker books of late—but to this day (she's attained the ripe old age of six as I write) she goes to these places for a slew of experiences, not simply the ones adults have in mind.

One morning when she was three, she asked how to spell *alligator*. She had often stared at a very lazy one at the zoo and seen pictures of others. She had an alligator bath toy. She was read stories and poems about them, along with dozens of other animals. She still asks adults around her to draw a picture of the animal interest of the moment, something we do dutifully if not particularly well; I am generally more pleased with my alligators than my cows, for example. She thought "see you later, alligator" was funny. She wasn't reading yet; she said she was too little, but she'd been spelling her name and a few others for months, and one morning, all of a sudden, she wanted to know how to spell *alligator*.

Let's connect the dots: a child sees something—say, an alligator—in her environment or in pictures of many sorts. It's given a name—a set of sounds she gradually associates with that thing. It's talked about and/or sung about in children's songs. By looking at books, she gets the concept that combinations of letters add up to particular words, and now she wants to write out ones that interest her.

There are at least two strands of note here. First, Wyla, like all kids, observes and interacts with the world directed by her own drive and employing those amazing tools with which most of us are born—our eyes and ears. Second, to help her sort out and think about these self-directed discoveries, parents and teachers supply a variety of assists, such as talking to her, identifying what interests her, and looking at books together.

A version of this is what happens during VTS lessons. As students' eyes scrutinize works of art, they find what interests them and search for words to express observations of all sorts—simple to complex—and the meanings, ideas, and emotions they draw from figures, interactions, settings, gestures, expressions, even colors. They find words to make subtle distinctions, language rarely employed day to day. As their ideas become more complicated, they are driven toward more complex vocabulary and sentences.

What kids see and think is amazing, though they often need and deserve help in expressing it clearly. Importantly, students are aided in the search for the words and the means to express them clearly by listening to their peers talk about the same subjects; such peer interactions cannot be overestimated as a learning assist. Of course, teachers extend this learning as they paraphrase student comments, sometimes adding needed vocabulary, modeling correct language usage, and ideally giving coherent form to ideas that are often expressed in a jumble.

In the preceding chapter we looked at the thinking contained in writing, linked it to elements of VTS facilitation, and considered a method for assessing the thinking/writing we've seen develop. We also pulled back to look at the writing expected of young people given existing standards as well as new ones. In this chapter we'll survey the bigger picture of why VTS might assist language development, including some of the theory that helps illuminate why VTS discussions could lead to growth in verbal ability.

SOME THEORY REGARDING LANGUAGE

I'm no expert in language development, but I think about it a great deal and read what I can. The subject is complicated, fascinating, and relevant to anyone working with children, and in my view of it, children are all "developing language" throughout elementary school. In order to understand the cognition involved in it, I have found the theories of a few scholars particularly helpful. I usually read bits of their research and theory at a time, seeking to understand something in particular, mostly to confirm or disabuse myself of a notion I've concluded based on my own observations. Simplifying and generalizing from this is a fool's task; be forewarned that what I say wouldn't pass academic muster. But, being a fool, I trudge onward anyway, citing (however well or badly) the work of others that helps explain the impact of VTS discussions on language.

One psychologist I have found to be insightful, as you know, is Rudolf Arnheim, who convinced me that the very act of seeing starts a process that, because of how our brains are wired, ends up helping us to form language. Our brains automatically begin a sorting process of what we see; in simple terms, we are wired for the perceptions to be transmitted to the parts of the brain that work to comprehend what we see and hear. Because we're humans, almost as instinctually, what is taken in and sorted out is routed to language centers of the mind; we begin to connect what we see to words we hear spoken by those around us. What we call *language ability* develops as a process that happens slowly over time, of course, and it happens with input from our environment: what we're encouraged to look at and what is said to us. The more of both, the better.

The most natural ways parents and early-childhood educators help infants learn to talk is, logically enough, by talking about what they see and do: "Here comes the spinach! It's green and warm and delicious! Let's eat and go outside for a walk to see what we can see . . . Oh, there's an ant." Studies have shown the importance of this. Research that has tracked how much language infants hear from those around them indicates that word-rich environments—ones where kids are actually talked to a great deal—prepare children for school in ways that word-poor environments do not.[1]

Developmental scientist Lev Vygotsky focused a great deal on the formation and development of speech; he too saw it as a process of integrating what a child sees and does with interactions with speakers in her environment. "The child begins to perceive the world not only through his eyes but also through his speech," he wrote in his book *Mind in Society*,[2] suggesting their symbiotic relationship. In one set of studies, Vygotsky observed children as they set about accomplishing challenging tasks and noted how frequently they talked their way through them. He also noted that children could solve as-yet-untried problems with guidance that could come from adults, but also from "collaboration with more capable peers,"[3] as mentioned in chapter 4—that is, help from someone who is essentially the child's equal but skilled or knowledgeable is some additional way.

Every time I think about this I'm reminded of a day at the park with Wyla, you won't be surprised to hear. She was eighteen months old when I put her on a swing for the first time. She was okay with this as long as she kept me in her grip as I walked awkwardly backward and forward trying to let her "swing." I was completely unsuccessful at convincing her to let go of me and put her hands on the chains; she'd have none of it. Then she glanced over at a child a few months older sitting in the next swing and holding onto his chains as a parent gently pushed. She immediately put her hands on the chains, and off we went, Wyla having learned from him that it could be done and that it was safe. He was at that moment her "more capable peer"; try as I might have, I was not.

Vygotsky wrote at length about thought as well as language; one tenet of his beliefs was that neither perceptions nor words alone constitute thought, though both are necessary components. It's when they are combined in the process of making meaning that they become what we think of and seek as thought. (I am eclipsing a great deal of what Vygotsky told us based on his research, so I urge you to seek out his books and make your way through them. It is helpful to do this with a reading group, by the way, taking passages you find particularly interesting and/or confusing, making slides of the text, and "VTSing" them with colleagues. It's a great way to figure out what he tells us.)

Just these few simplified ideas helped me make sense of a phenomenon those of us studying VTS didn't foresee, perhaps because it was almost too obvious: VTS experience talking about complicated images has a spinoff impact on writing. Teachers were first to notice that students' interest in and ability to write were increased when the writing prompts were visual. When we began collecting writing samples taken post–VTS discussions, we found something else: discussions themselves have a further, direct benefit on the capacity to write. We saw this in the previous chapter.

What pieces can we put together to reason why this is so? First, we have the powerful eye/mind connection that has been much discussed already. The word *visual* says it all: because seeing is such a practiced and useful resource to us, it makes sense that having something visual to write about would be helpful.

Second, the particular qualities of art make it intriguing as a subject: the fortuitous melding of accessible imagery and puzzling meaning as well as subjects of human interest.

Third, the questions were derived from data about the developmental levels of children (and most adults) when it comes to making sense of art. As gentle assists from a teacher, the questions enable behaviors already in use by students or within close proximity to what they can do; they are developmentally appropriate, within what Vygotsky called the "zone of proximal development"[4]—that is, what's within developmental reach.

Fourth, we incorporate the collaboration of peers who are probably equal with regard to viewing skills but differently able in terms of the perspectives and life experiences they bring to bear on examinations. The language used by other students is recognizable and familiar, but they might also know words we don't and see and think something that we don't, providing direct access to new vocabulary and ideas.

Fifth, paraphrasing by the teacher provides an appropriate assist while slightly upping the ante: the teacher assures all students that they are heard and valued and also helps them express what's on their minds. He models language for their thoughts.

Sixth, the focus of VTS is on making meaning of the images—many possible meanings, in fact—the activity that, according to Vygotsky, creates thought: when we combine perceptions and words in the course of making meaning, thoughts are formed in language. Most of what I've read makes me think that Vygotsky would have been intrigued by how children examining and talking about art creates an arena for pushing their meaning-making capacities, and therefore their thinking and language.

The hundreds of writing samples we've collected document both what teachers noted and what a three-year U.S. Department of

Education–funded study in Miami[5] found: VTS-nurtured students showed significant differences from the control students who had no VTS. Among other things, the former group's test scores went up more than expected in both reading and math, something particularly dramatic in ELL students. The kinds of changes seen in writing were on display in chapter 4; the samples shown were taken as part of the Miami research.

It makes sense that discussions might affect language. Conversation is often limited at home, if only because so many parents work long hours and relaxed family time is rare. Discussion is a small part of most instruction, and yet if you haven't had the chance to talk expansively, it's hard to expect your writing to be what is hoped for. Maybe it's as simple as this: if you can say it, you probably can write it. And, of course, the opposite would then be true: if you can't say it, perhaps you can't expect yourself to be able to write it. This may be truer for children than adults, but it makes me wonder about adult communication as well: too many of us feel that writing is hard. Could this be one reason why? That we aren't able to articulate aloud at least some of what goes on our heads, mostly because we do it rarely?

WHAT DOES THIS MEAN TO TEACHERS?

Language arts teachers—in other words, all elementary educators and specialists who further assist students—are often the first in schools to appreciate VTS. Expected to teach both oral and written language, teachers have far more strategies to teach writing than approaches to encourage oral expression, and they see VTS as a natural way to get kids to practice articulating their thoughts. One such teacher, relatively new to teaching, has no trouble expressing his delight at his work with adolescents and the use of VTS.

During his four-year career in the Boston Public Schools, Michael Baulier has taught English language arts to all grades from seniors to freshmen, and has decided to settle in with the latter. He loves those entering high school, coming from a variety of schools and neighborhoods and setting off on their third round of schooling. He enjoys "witnessing them build relationships and their identities. English was always my favorite subject in high school and teaching English language arts has seamlessly developed into my passion."

Michael introduced VTS to his classes at the Edward M. Kennedy Academy for Health Careers in the fall of 2012 to help him achieve his primary goal: "to teach students skills that will help make them successful in college and beyond. No matter what career they choose, I want all students to become effective communicators."

Michael has found that VTS image discussions have supported both what he wants from students and what is expected of them in terms of standards in language arts. He describes what drew him to VTS as well as its early impact on his class:

> The thinking skills that VTS promotes align nicely with what an ELA teacher wants his students to be able to do: make a thoughtful claim about a text and support it with specific evidence. I also saw several commonalities between VTS and the ELA Common Core standards for reading and writing that Massachusetts recently adopted. Both Common Core and VTS are grounded in this idea of providing students with less up front (background knowledge, pre-teaching, etc.), and instead, allowing them to arrive at their own evidence-based conclusions.
>
> The impact of VTS is visible in the classroom, especially among students who are looking for a structure to express their ideas and build on the ideas of their peers. I've noticed that students are becoming more comfortable with the prompt questions as they now automatically cite evidence with their claims without me asking, "What do you see that makes you say that?" For students who already have a sense of structured discussions, they use sentence stems with more ease and fluidity by making statements like, "I disagree with Jonathan's observation of the figure to the left because . . . " Experiences like these convince me that VTS is a valuable tool for building confidence and language development.

As you doubtless remember, Marion Bageant is a classroom veteran at the Garfield School in Spokane. One of the first things she appreciated about VTS was its impact on listening, something we all hope to nurture, but find very hard to teach in any direct manner. Parents often have little luck in this endeavor too: the habit of listening rarely comes from being asked or told to do it. Rather, it develops from experiencing the benefits. Listening becomes germane when it's interesting to do it and when it's perceived as useful. Ever vigilant, Marion noticed her students listening to others, and beginning to appreciate the usefulness of paying attention to what others say, during VTS discussions.

Second graders typically also struggle with writing. During a recent school year, roughly a quarter of Marion's students had particular challenges as writers; they were recent émigrés. Given several years' experience with VTS, she chose to integrate VTS into her teaching in particular ways. We know how she does it with story problems in math. To help in language arts, she conducts image discussions every few weeks when she's able to give at least ninety minutes to the process. She facilitates roughly thirty-minute conversations about the two images provided by VTS for second-grade lessons.

You may recall from chapter 3 that her challenged and ELL students probably say nothing during the discussions, so the question for Marion was, "Can I find out if they are getting anything out of listening to the discussions by asking them to write?" She therefore decided to let the kids write about one or both images for as long as they want, usually thirty minutes, more if they need it. The kids choose the picture they want to write about and take to the writing with as much interest and energy as they do in the discussions. The few that need special help, such as scribing, get it. That doesn't include the ELL students.

Earlier, we examined a post-discussion dictation from Allen, one of Marion's noncontributing, severely challenged students. But to get a sense of what Marion discovered from her ELL students, we'll examine two pairs of writing samples based on observations of figures 5.1[6] and 5.2,[7] taken roughly two months apart. To maintain their authenticity,

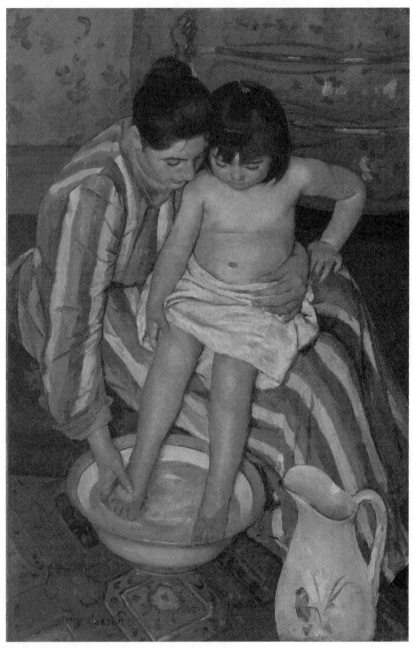

Figure 5.1

I've left the spelling and punctuation as they were and hope that you will look beyond those still-to-be-dealt-with aspects of writing and focus on the thinking and what it contributed to the writing more than technical issues. Although the students had VTS in kindergarten and first grade, the first writing sample was collected after the first VTS lesson in second grade, in late November, and the second after the fourth lesson, two months later.

Student 1

I notice that the mother is putting her douter legs in the bowl. And she wareing a towel. And I think something is going wronge because she putting her leg in the bowl And I think she got hurt and there are little red things in the water.

Student 2

I notice that the mom is washing the girl feet and the girl has a towel on her lap. The mom is holeing the [missing word: girl?] on her lap so she can wash her feet. I think the girl dad is outside with the boys.

Both of these students start with "I notice" (something probably heard in Marion's paraphrases) a mother/mom helping a girl/daughter put her feet into water—a complex observation. The second mentions that the girl is on her mother's lap to help the mother wash the girl's feet. Both point out that the girl is wearing a towel, adding detail to their first observation. Student 1 infers that "something's wrong," supplying evidence to back up her inference: "because she putting her leg in the bowl." She elaborates on this with the qualified "I think she got hurt" and adds a new detailed observation of "little red things in the water." Though she occasionally inserts periods and capital letters, the paragraph feels like a run-on sentence, and the last sentence is one.

Student 2 adds to a similar narrative he's constructed with an idiosyncratic inference: because there is no male in the picture, "the girl dad is outside with the boys." Though a *because* is missing, I'd argue that he's providing evidence for his first inference: it's because she's on the mom's lap that he therefore thinks the mom is washing the girl's feet. I'd call his first sentence compound because the second half adds a detail that elaborates on the subject of the first.

Neither of them has anything to say about the pitcher, the rug, and the setting (though it might be hard for them to recognize the dresser and other details of the room), nor does either provide any description of the mother.

Here are the second samples, this time based on figure 5.2, taken a scant two months later.

Student 1

I see a little girl rideing a brown horse. I think the horse is a girl. Because she's waring a crown and a neckleas. I thing the figer is looking for a home. To live in. I think she ran away from her house because she must be scared of her family. And she looking for a new house to live in. At the back I see the mountin is white. It must be snow. At the bottem I see some lake across and the lake is white.

Student 2

I think the boy is going on a journey because he is on a hourse. I think the boy is rich and he is a prince. I see a big sea by the montine. I think the boy lives by the montine hill. I saw a little island that is close to the sea. I think it stop raining. I also see a sun shining and a rainbow. I think the hourse is a girl because it has a nekklas and bow in her hair. I see a island fill with tree and little house and some dirt. I see the hourse wereing lot of gold and has curly hair and she is happy. I saw the montine fill with rocks and water. I see the sea is blue and I see the island is green and it has lots of grass in it. I saw the boy climing a dry monine and it has red thing on it.

In both of these samples, our ELL students create narratives, shaped from many of the same observations, but where the first samples were parallel in most ways, these are not. You can almost imagine in the first

Figure 5.2

instance what the discussion of the mother-and-child image covered, which wasn't much. But here the two students notice a great deal more, both pointing to many of the same features of the picture, yet also noticing different details and creating different stories, even disagreeing about the rider's gender—not unreasonably.

Both examine the whole picture and mention most of what is depicted throughout it, a big change from the first sample. Both include a number of "I think" sentences, indicating some level of awareness of the subjectivity of their interpretations. Both provide lots of detail for their many observations: the horse is brown, the mountain is white, the sea is blue; one island has a tree, a little house, and some dirt; another is green and has lots of grass; and so on. Both provide evidence for at least some of their inferences: the gender of the horse is determined by the necklace and crown/bow; the boy's on a journey because he's on a horse; because the mountain is white, there must be snow. Student 2 returns to the horse to add details about its curly mane and the gold in its harness; he also infers, without providing evidence, that the horse is happy.

Student 1 develops her narrative fairly completely and then proceeds to add a few final details about the setting. She uses the word *figure*, another term probably picked up from the teacher's paraphrase. Student 2 dispenses with his narrative in the first couple of sentences but fills out his lengthy statement with a rich supply of details, some harder to see than others—the rainbow, for example. The range of what he mentions, and the detail given, would make it possible to conjure up much of this scene simply from reading, not just what's depicted but what it looks like. I'm struck by the notion, probably surmised by his looking carefully at the coloration of the sky, that the rain has just stopped; this young man has the makings of a good descriptive writer.

These changes occurred within a very short span of time. As I mentioned, Marion says that for the most part these students listen to the discussions without participating. They are still learning English. They are only seven years old. They are considered at-risk, and have few advantages outside of school. Yet they show measurable growth. I think this gives us much to think about.

Perhaps Marion has a special sensitivity to such students because she emigrated herself as a young person, and she told me something that I'd never thought about before: many English language learners are reluctant to join in conversation not so much because they don't have the vocabulary, but because they fear that they won't make themselves understood or, worse, that they'll be laughed at for saying something the wrong way. Marion hypothesizes that, among other things, as words take shape in the minds of ELL students, they will, at first, conform to the pattern of language native to students' mother tongues, and constructions might sound odd if expressed in English.

When hearing this I was reminded of a lyric of a song, sung by Patti Page, from my long-ago youth: "Throw mama from the train a kiss, a kiss . . ." The song was produced as a novelty, but when hearing Marion talk about ELL kids and why they're reluctant to speak up, I began to realize that we were laughing at someone's expense when we found this way of speaking goofy.

In Marion's kinder and more informed view, VTS offers several supports for those still acquiring language, a process that goes on throughout the elementary grades even for native English speakers. The attributes she cites echo to some extent the list of possible connections I enumerated earlier. But there's an important difference: Marion is a trained and accomplished teacher of ELL students. My points were theorized from observation, reading, and thought. Hers represent practice—real life—more than theory.

The first reason for this progress is that the prompt is visual: the children can see what they are discussing. Since the teacher continuously points to what is observed, she anchors the spoken comments in imagery. Students can keep their eyes on what's being discussed.

Second, as students contribute comments, others listen avidly, probably drawn in by the act of puzzling meaning from pictures; they, too, are interested in figuring out what's going on. They hear their peers describe what they see and what they think about it, speaking as the kids they are, developmentally within reach of other students.

Third, the teacher paraphrases each comment, providing vocabulary and verbal syntax to reinforce the language experience. She models good language usage.

The fourth building block is one integrated by many teachers, and is used especially well by Marion: the chance to write. With both the image and conversation fresh in their minds, students move from speaking to writing, and the continuous activity becomes its own support for language development. This is also a way of moving from a teacher-facilitated peer discussion to individual activity, from group effort with teacher-supplied prompts to operating on one's own without help.

Marion gives her students as much time as they want to write—usually between twenty and thirty minutes—and therefore each has the opportunity to sort out and express the observations and ideas he took away from the experience. Conveniently, the writing serves as a record of a student's language capacities at that moment, and a context for displaying what each sees, how he describes it, and what it means to him, a full circuit of perception to meaning making.

Marion is very clear about the power of this process and feels that it's allowing all of her second graders to become successful writers. When most typically wrote only a few words during their initial forays into writing at the beginning of the school year, within a few months they are comfortable writing whenever she asks. The impact of this on tests will eventually be seen, but the (in my estimation) quite ambitious Washington State standards seek this:

> In second grade, students make significant progress as they move from single-idea and patterned sentences to more detailed and sequential text, often including more than one event or descriptive element. Students demonstrate a considered approach to their writing by planning purposefully and working toward accuracy and effectiveness by making some conscious word choices. Sentence structures are varied within a single piece of writing. Students write in a variety of forms, including nonfiction, while maintaining the basic conventions of writing. Students notice mistakes while rereading and revise by adding details.[8]

Even these midyear samples from ELL students suggest they are on their way to meeting these goals.

Craig Madison expresses ideas similar to Marion's given his multi-year experience with VTS at El Verano Elementary School, where most students hear very little English at home, if any. He reflects on pairs of "before and after" VTS writing samples by third graders as follows:

> *In my opinion, the change is not just a result of the natural maturing process and/or a typical language arts curriculum. As we have seen at El Verano, the use of VTS throughout the year accounts for at least 50 percent of the improvement. VTS has allowed the students to look and think long on a topic, which has allowed time for patterns to emerge for them. The building of meaning as a community has been developed to such an extent by the end of third grade, that students are able to independently apply the skill without their companions. As a result, they produce writing with vastly improved descriptions when compared to their start-of-the-year attempts.*
>
> *There are exceptions: kids who are at Beginner and Early Intermediate CELDT [California English Language Development Tests] levels show improvement, but it isn't dramatic. With these kids, we see excellent progress in moving from purely concrete observations to more details and inferences with evidence.*

Tracy McClure, writing about students in her nearby school with fewer non-English-speaking families, echoes these observations:

> *It is hard to separate a growth in maturity, added writing instruction incorporated, and VTS experiences when trying to assess the writing. My hunch is that the change in the number of observations included, the evidence provided, and the multiple interpretations are all part of growth directly related to VTS.*
>
> *When simply comparing the pre and post writing samples, the growth is absolutely remarkable—the growth in writing is evident, but it is the growth in thinking that I find especially compelling, and that thinking is very VTS.*

As you know, Tracy has integrated not only VTS image discussions into her classes but also poetry discussions. I asked her if she thought that this in-depth experience with literature had any additional impact on students' writing. While we were discussing this, she went to her files to find a writing assignment not directly related to either images or poetry, something that might show us what students internalize because of a range of instruction and experience as little influenced by the teacher as possible. She found one: as a graduation requirement, California sixth graders have to write a "Response to Literature." Teachers might give counsel to make sure students understand the assignment itself, but they are not allowed to edit or make suggestions concerning what the students write. Here are the instructions, copied directly from the Internet:[9]

Response to Literature five-paragraph format
Part 1/Paragraph 1 (may be more than one paragraph long)—Summary
Summarize the book by giving information about these parts:

- Beginning (title, author, main characters, setting, and main problem or conflict)
- Middle (tell about two or three events around the main conflict)
- End (tell the resolution/dénouement)

Part 2/Paragraph 2—Judgment about character or event, supported with relevant facts from story
A judgment is a statement about a character or event in the book; there is no right or wrong judgment as long as the judgment can be supported by the text and makes sense

Part 3/Paragraph 3—Prediction related to judgment, supported with relevant story evidence
Predict what might happen if events in the story were different or predict what REALISTICALLY might happen in the future if the story continued

Part 4/Paragraph 4—Supporting the judgment with a connection and relevant story evidence

There are three types of connections:

- Text to self—comparing something in the book with something in your life
- Text to world—comparing events in the book to world events
- Text to text—comparing events in the book to another book you have read

In your writing, do not announce to your reader that you are making a connection and do not name the connection type. Your connection should flow smoothly and be an organic part of the piece.

Part 5/Paragraph 5—Conclusion with interpretation *(what was the author's point/what is the life-skill message) and opinion of the book*

- Make a concluding statement about the book/wrap it up
- Include a hint about your interpretation and then fully develop the interpretation and support it with evidence from the text

Interpretations could include these:

- identifying the author's message
- identifying the book's theme/or life-skill message
- understanding what the author is trying to teach us
- End with your opinion of the story

This is virtually the opposite of a free write. From the results, you know almost as much about whether or not a student can follow instructions as about how she writes or thinks about a book. You don't learn what a student might do with a more open-ended prompt to demonstrate what she has learned about "responding to literature." In any case, here is a Response to Writing by a high-achieving student (not designated gifted but hard-working and successful) in the spring of 2007, before VTS was introduced to Old Adobe, chosen from Tracy's files:

Stargirl

Follow Leo. A student at Mica High in Arizona, as he tells you about his confusing high school days in Stargirl by Jerry Spinelli. As he meets Stargirl, the unusual new kid with the rat, he falls in love as the book progresses. But as he starts getting "buddy buddy" with her, he starts getting ignored by everyone else. Now he has to choose between love and popularity.

Leading up to his choice, Leo goes through a lot of events and learns about himself. He has a show called Hot Seat, goes on adventures and sees a different side of Stargirl. When he finally makes his choice, his decision is cemented and there is no turning back.

I believe that Stargirl is a caring person, kind at heart, and a loving friend. She is always thinking of others. She makes cards for any occasion, and for people she doesn't know. She sings to people on their birthday, and also sends gifts to people who need cheering up. Overall, I think that Stargirl makes an awesome friend.

I think that if Leo chose Stargirl over everyone else, she might not have moved. The Ocotillo Ball wouldn't have been as fun and memorable because Stargirl would have had a date. If Leo would have chosen Stargirl, everything would have been different.

In this book, Stargirl stood out as the new kid. The same thing happened to me, but with gymnastics instead of school. I stood out like a black sheep in a heard of white sheep for a while, but after a week or so, I became friends with everyone.

To conclude, Stargirl by Jerry Spinelli is a great book that sends a message that people should remember and take to heart . . . Be yourself!! You shouldn't change yourself for somebody else's benefit if you are not happy with it. Be who you are and show it off to the world. Be yourself and love it!

Here is another from spring 2011 by another high achiever (also not labeled gifted), but this one had VTS with images for four years as well as Tracy's "poem a day" discussions during the entire sixth-grade year:

A Bad Case of Stripes

A Bad Case of Stripes *by David Shannon is like an orchestrated piece of music, with high notes and low notes, all resulting in a pleasant closing. Through different bars in the piece, Camilla is trying to resolve the predicament she is in. Whether being at school or her home, she can't find a solution to her bad case of stripes. The only problem besides her stripes is that Camilla will not eat lima beans, a food she relishes, because she wants to blend in with all the other children, who despise lima beans.*

One morning, Camilla awoke engulfed in a rainbow of stripes. Camilla loathed the thought of having to go to school; she would stand out like a red thumb, and Camilla wanted the exact opposite. Since Camilla wasn't under the weather, she was coerced to go to school because she was only blanketed in a pattern. Shortly after Camilla arrived to school, all her peers began to badger her, behaving like laughing hyenas, and shouting out patterns to shift the design on Camilla. Camilla was obliged to stay home from school since her stripes could be contagious. Meanwhile, experts and specialists came, but neither the specialists nor the experts could find a remedy for Camilla's bad case of stripes. While Camilla has been transformed into the walls of her bedroom, an elderly woman comes to feed Camilla lima beans. Once Camilla finally agrees to consume the lima beans, she turns back into her typical self.

Camilla wanted to assimilate to all the other children by not being true to herself. Camilla was taking drastic measures to ensure that on the first day of school, she would dress to impress all her fellow classmates. Camilla wouldn't even eat lima beans, a food she loved, because all of her friends were disgusted by the beans. When Camilla first awoke in stripes, she was dreading going to school since too much attention would emerge upon her. Instead of worrying about what the other kids thought, Camilla should have been her sincere self.

If the story continued, Camilla might be teased for eating lima beans, but people might start to like them. Perhaps Camilla would start a lima bean trend if other students were as Camilla once was and wanted to be like all of their peers. Conversely, Camilla could be pestered by the other children because nobody else enjoyed lima beans. Although what would matter most was that Camilla was being herself so she wouldn't have another bad case of stripes.

Camilla was diffident. I was also once a sheepish adolescent who wanted to be like twins with my friend. I paid far too much attention to her likes when I should have been more attentive to myself. For example, on the first day of school, I would fret about how if I didn't dress like my friend, she might not like me anymore. That is similar to how Camilla was making a great fuss about her outfit for the first day of school. I would also worry about drawing attention to myself in a negative way. For instance, Camilla never wanted to stand out, only to mix in completely with all her peers. Lastly, I would always listen to what my classmates told me and just stand there defenseless like Camilla only stood there when the children shouted patterns at her.

To conclude this melodious segment, the moral of the story is not to merge into a mold people create for you, but to be unique in your own way. The sheets of music could be saying that if you keep trying to be like everyone else, you might lose yourself along with your own special melody. The author could be teaching us about making our own music as we go along and reminding us not to follow a tune that was written for us. The author could be telling us not to worry about what others think, but to be ourselves. David Shannon could be saying that we need to dance like no one is watching.

Here are the criteria that must be met for successful completion of this assignment. Students are given this list alongside the detailed instructions:

Engages the reader with a known strategy

Summarizes the story

Makes a judgment and supports it with relevant evidence

Provides a prediction that refers to the text

Provides a connection with the text

Has a concluding statement that is an interpretation of the text and that includes your opinion of the book

Uses transition words or expressions

Includes at least five examples of vivid language

Is organized into paragraphs that progress in a logical sequence

Includes at least three complex sentences that are correctly punctuated

Has all no excuse words [a list of simple words students have no excuse for not spelling and using correctly] and conventions correct

Has exemplary presentation (neat writing that is pleasant to read)[10]

Both students did a creditable job meeting each criterion, although neither piece of literature, in my opinion, set a very high bar for comprehension, compared, say, to an Emily Dickinson poem. The language of the first student wasn't particularly vivid and his punctuation isn't perfect, and this might have affected his overall score, but he generally achieved what was expected. So did other students; it was hard choosing among available examples to find two that were "typical" of "before VTS" or "after VTS plus poem a day." But it wasn't hard to see the contrast between the two sets. (Remember, both of these students had Tracy as their teacher, and both are generally successful in school. The difference between the two is the amount of discussion they had about art and poetry—one a little, one a lot.) So what are the differences between the writing outcomes?

The second writer has more to say and logically enough writes a longer statement, more than twice the length of the first. This would mean little if the content weren't worth the extra words, but it is. Though both repeat certain ideas and even phrases, the second does it less and, when she does, it seems related to the assignment; what's the difference between "identifying the author's message," "identifying the book's theme/or life-skill message," and "understanding what the author is trying to teach us," for example? I'd be hard-pressed to make clear distinctions without some repetition.

The first sample leaves me a bit confused about many complicating details of the story: events, character traits, and plot developments are mentioned incompletely, so while I get the drift of the story, I am left wondering about various events/conflicts such as the Ocotillo Ball and whether Stargirl went or not, as well as what happened to either of the protagonists in the end.

With sample two, I feel as if I've read the book; the student provides a good summary near the beginning and later adds useful details, fleshing out both the story line and the feel of the book itself. That said, both students seem to understand and convey the overall messages contained in the different books.

The first student's writing is lively and readable. His opening two-word sentence is arresting: "Follow Leo." However, the next sentence, while it qualifies the "Follow Leo," isn't complete. At first I thought he did something stylistically interesting, but I concluded that he still doesn't completely understand grammar and punctuation. His overuse of commas argues for that conclusion too. There's no such problem with the second student, who clearly has command of both; she even uses a semicolon correctly.

Part of what makes the first sample easy to read is the vocabulary. He uses vernacular and gives the impression of being very comfortable writing. Our second writer is considerably more adventurous, using many words that add color (part of how she evokes the tone of the book): *orchestrated, predicament, relishes, despise, engulfed, loathed, coerced, blanketed, badger, obliged, transformed, consume*—all within the first two paragraphs. She uses neither/nor correctly. She describes the main character as *diffident* later in the essay, and I was unsure if it meant what she thought it did. I looked it up, and sure enough, *insecure*—the word I might have chosen—is one of its definitions. She's definitely aware that vocabulary enriches text, yet she folds evocative word choices into a straightforward, unpretentious essay, adding interest, flavor, and intelligence to the writing.

The second student ambitiously begins and ends her essay with a simile. It might seem forced in the first paragraph, but when she cycles back to it in the last, she applies the strategy compellingly. She introduces a new metaphor with her last line (dance instead of music), but she's invoking appropriate associations to underscore her point, and in my view it works. She forgets to give her opinion of the book explicitly, though it's not hard to see that, like the first student, she enjoyed it.

When following the instructions to sum up the author's message in the last paragraph, the first writer seems sure and unequivocal: Be yourself! And he's probably right about *Stargirl*, the book he encapsulates. David Shannon's intent in *A Bad Case of Stripes* could be summarized in an equally straightforward manner, but the second student gives it many shades of possibility. In each of the five sentences where she summarizes what she thought the author *might be* saying, she interprets the message differently, allowing for more readings. She adds layers of complexity; yes, the book might be summed up in one declarative sentence as the first student did, but in her more complicated way of writing, she gives us the readers the impression of greater depth, both to the story and incidentally to her.

IN SUMMARY

I hope you will come to your own conclusions about the relative merits of these two samples. But what I want you to keep in mind is that, however you assess them, the differences are the result of Tracy shifting her strategies. She was a constant factor over the years, and we know that teachers matter; they directly impact student achievement. But less talked about is their teaching. A shift in method was likely the main cause of the significant differences between the two.

It's sobering for me to think that Tracy's students (and Marion's, and Craig's) experienced the same dedicated, caring, creative teacher over the years, yet when these teachers shift strategies to include discussion as a key instructional element, kids' performances improve. When the teachers introduce them to complex imagery and literature and let students explore it, coming to terms with it as they will given who they are, it boosts the capacities of those students beyond what more teacher- or subject-centric methods achieve.

CHAPTER 6

Learning How "to VTS"

WHEN WAS THE LAST TIME you said to yourself, "I know . . . I'll use art to help bring my struggling writers up to speed!"

Few of us operate with such notions in mind, and while there's talk about how the arts bolster academic achievement, it's not something we actually see in many schools or classrooms. This might be in part because proof that art experience has a significant impact on what kids are supposed to learn in school is scant. Few interventions have been shown to cause growth in concrete skills such as reading and writing or the acquisition of particular information. This is not to say that the arts *don't* have an impact, just that the data proving it is scarce, and seldom are the relationships "causal," meaning that the arts intervention reliably caused "academic" learning and will predictably do so again when repeated.

As a case in point, only part of what I've written about VTS-related impact has been studied in a controlled, scientific way by Abigail Housen and Karin DeSantis and corroborated by other robust studies. Thus, only some of the thinking behaviors are documented in hard data, and the relationship between thinking and writing is conjectural. While from looking at writing samples, we can hypothesize VTS's impact on writing as a craft—it seems obvious—it has never been analyzed in a dispassionate, clinical way. It's like the learning monitored by the teachers at El Verano: visible and very likely true, but not proven. This is another topic that could be addressed by scholarly means and provide useful arguments to those of us who seek to help all kids in ways that diverge from the norms.

Meanwhile, the place of the arts in schools has been marginal for so long, few of us grow up remembering much more than marching bands, scronky orchestras, holiday concerts for beaming parents, poster contests, and a few super-talented kids who could sing, dance, or draw well. But to the extent that these were part of our lives, they were usually extracurricular activities, and rare were the incursions of the arts into the classroom, where the "important" work was done. Most of us wrote a few poems at some point in language arts. And we went on the occasional museum field trip, though many such opportunities have fallen by the wayside as more "basic" needs have been stressed and money for education has diminished. It's no surprise, therefore, that collectively we seldom conceive of the arts as addressing core learning objectives, those by which teachers are judged effective or not.

So then I come along and say, "Here's this VTS thing that uses discussions of art to produce measureable learning in thinking and language." It might well be a little hard to accept: how could this work? Despite uneven results from direct instruction, it's a challenge to imagine that free-ranging discussions of images could propel kids toward reaching prioritized goals that elude conventional teaching practices. VTS can feel like a foreign practice. It's "indirect" and can seem as if it's not teaching. The powerful influence of time-tested instruction, combined with little insight into how art can be "useful" and compounded by the relative rarity of discussions as serious teaching, make it hard to believe that VTS can help accomplish the learning we all want to see, much less the achievement teachers have been assigned to effect.

In this chapter, I introduce the process by which we've learned to address underlying skepticism about VTS and its impact. What follows describes the professional development model we've crafted to give teachers space, time, and support as they grapple with various dilemmas, ones we all have to one degree or another.

MORE HISTORY, AND SOME RATIONALE

I certainly had my own doubts about VTS as we experimented with it. I knew I needed to recast my own teaching after the bad news we received at MOMA, but still I questioned the impact VTS would have. Even acknowledging that I'd forgotten most of what I'd learned in school, including college, it was hard to fathom that discussions would make an appreciable difference. Throughout my education, I experienced only conventional forms of teaching, and as a result believed that sharing what I learned over time and effort was a critical aspect of teaching. I presumed that correcting mistakes and directing students' work were necessary to learning no matter what age or stage I was teaching. When I first started to use VTS as my main teaching tool, I sometimes felt fraudulent. If I were demonstrating VTS to other professionals, I felt the urge to say, "But you know this isn't the only way I know how to teach. You should see me . . ."

So let's think about this for a bit. I went on at some length in the preceding chapters to describe the attributes of art that make it attention grabbing and compelling to talk about, why discussions of it impact thinking, and how thinking in turn affects writing. But my writing about it, however convincingly I argue the case, might not resonate so clearly when it comes to actually fitting VTS into schedules that barely leave teachers space to breathe. With little time for anything beyond curricula in language arts and math, and some months taken over by test preparation, how can a teacher have confidence that such a detour from mandated instruction is actually going to push the prioritized agenda forward?

The only way I know to overcome skepticism about the usefulness of art is to become more personally connected to it than most of us are, and the best way I know to do that is how the kids do it: experience VTS discussions of art with peers. Teachers need time to examine something they've never seen before (or revisit something they have), noodle through what is familiar with other adults, puzzle over ambiguities, voice their thoughts and quandaries, and feel engaged by differing observations and ideas.

To appreciate VTS, we need to know the rush that comes from collective discoveries. We need the insights of other adults to close the gap between us and objects sequestered in museums, where we might think they exist in a realm apart. Looking hard and thinking deeply about art is the way to develop a bond with it. We not only gain insight into why art engages our students but also move beyond apprehension that we need special knowledge to engage with it, the knowledge that MOMA visitors thought we could simply hand over to them.

And yet another point: while we engage in VTS discussions about art, it's hard not to bond with those with whom we are sharing our ideas. We are talking about an art object but revealing what it means to us. It works in two directions: as we listen to others, we learn about them. As we share observations and meanings, the respectful way we engage in meaningful conversations with peers often makes many other communications easier and more productive. VTS discussions among teachers can and often do create a sense of community within a school culture, something most appreciate.

Through discussions with our peers, we also experience the benefits of VTS as a teaching/learning strategy. When we learn what it takes to make ourselves speak up, or, on the other hand, feel the irrepressible urge to share some observation or idea, we gather what VTS demands of eyes and minds, and the opportunity it provides. When we personally feel the encouragement of someone not just listening to us but also proving she understands what we say—when we hear our ideas validated in someone else's voice and language—we begin to grasp the value of paraphrasing. When we witness an idea of ours linked to others, whether in agreement or not, we understand the impact of listening as well as the ease given to rigorous debate that comes from VTS facilitation. When we indulge in the pleasure of open-ended exploration ourselves, it's easier to accommodate the unpredictability of VTS discussions. When we feel the gratification that comes from pursuing ideas and issues that mean something to us in a thoughtful way, we rediscover the benefits of a discovery process. When we see a number of people who use the same questions and strategy but whose own personalities show through, we realize we're not being handed another restrictive script.

When introducing VTS to our students and listening to them share their observations and ideas, we learn a great deal about them—often things we did not know—and they about each other. As facilitators, we find out what matters to them and how they see; through listening, and with the help of paraphrasing and linking, we get snapshots of their thinking and language and also insights into what they know. And the better we are at facilitation, the more we learn.

This brings us back to the importance of image discussions with our peers: as our own thinking about images gets richer from examining and discussing more of them, we more easily follow the often-complicated things that come out of kids' mouths, particularly as their viewing skills advance. We need our own conversations in order to keep up with theirs.

In other words, the best way to come to believe in the value of VTS is to experience many image discussions and to pull back and share what we learn from each other and the process. Similarly, the best way to understand its impact on students is to engage in VTS conversations with them *and* habitually reflect on what we observe. When we rethink what happens during discussions—whether of images or other topics—we not only consider what we might do to improve our practice but also make more and more sense of what students are learning. We set ourselves up to be able to assess thinking and writing in new ways.

Learning VTS is a matter of practice and reflecting on that practice, something most productively done with colleagues going through the same process. Reflecting with peers allows us to talk things out, problem-solve together, and scaffold off each other's insights and abilities—in precisely the way that students learn from VTS. As it happens, this shared and deliberated process is a model for the kind of interactions required for schools striving to find their own ways to achieve Common Core standards.

What follows is a synopsis of what we've learned about learning VTS.

LEARNING VTS

VTS is a pretty simple strategy, but most people adopting it find it's not quite as easy as it first appears. VTS uses different skills from those required for other instruction or those we put to use in our daily lives. During image discussions, for example, we have to listen harder than normal, concentrating intensely to follow and remember all that is said. We can't be double-tasking, handing out work sheets or mashing the potatoes while we half-listen to someone's tales of his day. Pointing to pertinent places in the images mentioned as students speak actually helps us stay focused and remember what is said.

We must also quickly process what we hear and find new language with which to paraphrase it, exercising our own language skills creatively. We must continue to reflect on our feet—operating in meta-cognition—to link similar and disparate ideas as well as chart the unfolding scaffold of ideas.

Why all of these skills matter can be grasped quickly on one level, but understanding is increased as we watch students. Improved practice usually comes from noticing how a skillful paraphrase affects a student we particularly want to support. It also results from serious and extended consideration of the paradigm involved in this form of teaching and learning, something that becomes more meaningful when the results are witnessed, not described or read about. Even teachers who hit the ground running find that their skills improve over time and practice, especially once the questions become second nature, listening intently becomes easier, and the possibilities for helping with language and clarifying thinking become apparent. Observing others as well as being observed and coached also make a marked difference.

Skepticism about VTS (or any other teaching strategy) is a useful thing. I'm convinced that a healthy interrogation of new ideas is wise. And the same might be said of conventional methods: wouldn't it be smart to examine their validity from time to time? Just because we do something routinely, does it work as we assume it does? I'm pretty sure that VTS would be half what it is if those of us working on it hadn't become imbued with the instinct to say, "Yes, but . . ." or "Hmmm. Not sure. What's the evidence?"

Acknowledging all of this, there are three prongs to the VTS professional development process we've evolved over twenty years to help people learn it; for the sake of brevity, I'm going to refer to this as *training*. The first prong is demonstration, (mostly live but sometimes by way of tapes of people teaching), followed by analytical discussions. The second is practice facilitating VTS lessons. The third is examining that experience: reflecting what we see happening both to us and to our students. Questions and discussion are the backbones of instruction. My summary of this, again, is "practice and reflect on that practice with one's peers."

On the VTS Web site we provide a good deal of information, such as research data, but it's there to augment practical experience and to support individuals who seek to know something because they've become curious. Even data about the impact of VTS is relevant only when it illuminates what you wonder about from watching your students, when an issue becomes your question.

VTS training begins with a very brief introduction and then immediately proceeds to a demonstration, after which the demonstrator asks, "How was that for you as a learner?" giving everyone a chance to discuss what it might be like for one's students. Usually another demonstration, ideally by a different person, follows, and after this the trainer asks, "What did I do as facilitator?" As each element of VTS is identified, a follow-up question is posed: "What was the purpose of that?" The assembled group then discusses the function of that element: what learning objectives the element is designed to affect. For example, participants might say, "You asked questions," and once the wording of each is precisely noted, participants put their heads together to come up with what learning is intended by asking questions in general as well as by each specific question. Even the wording is analyzed and alternatives evaluated.

Meanwhile, VTS trainers facilitate the process just as they do in image discussions, paraphrasing what's said; the right answers to the questions are the ones that participants brainstorm. After all, they're teachers; they have a huge range of experience among them to apply to thinking about the learning intended in, say, "What do you see that makes you say that?" This form of group analysis is a common practice throughout VTS training.

After this group effort has made its first stab at deconstructing VTS, practice begins: participants break into small groups to try VTS, and as each demonstrator finishes, we introduce our means of coaching— what we call the *coaching formula.*

Coaching involves—no surprise—a set of questions that provides a structure for helping teachers explore the practice and help each other in a way that mirrors student-centered teaching; it's guided but leaves the thinking and content up to the teachers. After someone demonstrates, he is asked the first question, "What did you learn from and/or how did you feel about this teaching?" He is given a chance to think about and report to the group about what he experienced, before any feedback from the group. It's one thing to watch others teach, but quite another to try it oneself, and this question gives the demonstrator an immediate chance to talk about what he experienced, thought about, and felt while trying VTS the first (or second, or third, etc.) time.

As in VTS discussions, the coach will paraphrase the demonstrator's comments to make sure that all thoughts and feelings are acknowledged, and then turns to the group to ask, "What did you learn from and what did you appreciate about our demonstrator's teaching?" We phrase it this way to remind ourselves that teacher/student exchanges are best if they start out with something positive. It's worth remembering that our relationships with students are always imbued with emotions: teachers project feelings, and students respond to those and have their own. Yes, we try to be dispassionate and objective and even-handed, but everything we do as teachers matters on an emotional plane as well. Our smiles or frowns, our choice of words, our tone of voice, and our gestures all convey subtle meanings that are read by our students, and we should hope that they help put them at ease and encourage them to engage. By asking this coaching question, we invite participants to provide positive feedback, couched in terms of what they enjoyed about another's teaching.

(As I wrote that thought, I remembered that, were we in the midst of training, I'd most likely pose the question, "Does this make sense?" and I'd really want you to respond. I'd want to know what you thought about what I just said. So consider that for a minute before you read on. *Does* the notion that it's important to give feedback in terms of what behaviors are appreciated by the students make sense to you?)

Getting back to coaching, the next question posed specifically relates to the skepticism that I think should be automatic among teachers: "Was anyone surprised by anything?" The question asks participants to think about any expectations they might have had coming into the experience that were not met, or vice versa: things that happened that were not anticipated. It's pretty hard for us to go into any experience without assumptions and expectations about how it's going to work and how students will perform. We can't avoid it and it's not by definition bad; high expectations can boost students' own. But to make sure that expectations limit neither us nor our students, we need to review lessons in retrospect to see if our expectations (often articulated concretely by way of lesson objectives) were reasonable: was the subject a good one and the discussion insightful? Did I reach my objectives? Fall short? Did students exceed them? What about outliers—students who did less well than the norm, ones who were clearly challenged, and others who might have excelled to a degree not expected?

Based on this assessment, I can decide what to do either to make up for what didn't happen or to build on the capacities I didn't expect, planning the next lesson so that I consistently offer needed support and/or adequate challenge to all students.

My shorthand for this process of review is taking the "stance of the skeptic"—assuming as little as possible, willingly examining and reexamining what I do as a teacher, knowing what my expectations are and thinking about the actual results. When I experience something I don't expect, I have to figure out how to take advantage of good news or make up for losses. This is hard to do when curricula are mandated, but when we have choices (as with VTS, and as we will need to make as we consider how to reach Common Core standards), we should make the most of it.

The next step in coaching involves something that turns out to be quite difficult: phrasing criticism as questions. It's very direct to say to someone, "You did this wrong," or "You didn't do that right," but what is the person criticized supposed to do then? Become defensive is one possibility; when caught short, especially in front of our peers, it's hard not to. But even if we accept the comment with composure, we probably weren't aware of what we did wrong and we might not know how to fix it once it's pointed out.

To avoid this kind of dead end, we ask teachers to incorporate critical comments in a question. Let's say a novice demonstrator phrased the second question, "What made you say that?" The trainer is likely to model the questioning process by saying, "As I watched, you made me think of a question. What's the difference between asking, 'What made you say that?' and the VTS second question, 'What did you *see* that made you say that?'" At a later moment, when a teacher is still learning but has built up more confidence, and the group notices she has left out key observations or ideas when paraphrasing, relevant questions might be phrased something like, "What happens if we paraphrase only part of what someone said?" Or, "Why do we want children to know we understand and accept all they say?" Or, "What can we do to keep track of all that a student says?" (And by the way, how would you answer these questions?)

At this point in coaching, it's not as if the demonstrator doesn't realize she's being called on something she missed in terms of para-phrasing—something she didn't get quite right. Of course she knows. But because she's been asked a question, she has a chance to think about why we paraphrase and why we try to capture all that was said, rather than simply to dwell on the mistake. To help the process along, the coach opens the discussion for suggestions and perspectives from others, too, so that together the group noodles through to a greater un-derstanding of paraphrasing.

This form of critique emphasizes that learning to facilitate isn't a matter of getting it right. We're not seals learning to honk horns. We're trying a method out, and when we fall short (as we probably will), it's good to acknowledge our misstep but not to feel the sting of failure, however modest. I think that nurture always beats out anything con-strued as a reprimand in learning whether the student is in kinder-garten, graduate school, or VTS training. Learning how to help others think about the implications of their behavior in this positive manner can be one of the biggest side benefits of learning VTS. Framing what you want someone to think about through questions is not easy, but it's worth the effort. I've even seen it ease tension in my personal life. And coming up with the right question is at the heart of good teaching, especially when the goal is activating the learning process in students, as the teachers described in chapter 4 are trying to do—and as we must do to meet Common Core standards.

Nurture, in my view, is underrated in education, and misplaced em-phasis on discipline or rigor just makes many students feel inadequate. As I see it, good performance of any task comes not from following a rule, but from understanding the function of the rule. I don't text while driving, not because of the law—I'm willing to exceed the speed limit, after all—but because I've seen that it's dangerous. I'll work on my paraphrasing when I've become convinced that the tool shows students I listen to them, remember all they say, and understand them, and that this feedback directly affects their willingness to engage and learn. (Again, were we meeting together, I'd likely reinsert the question, "Does this makes sense?" It's a tic, I guess, but I don't want you to take anything for granted or as truth. I want you to think about how this jibes with your values and experience. Stay skeptical, remember?)

Meanwhile, to finish the coaching discussion and provide closure for the demonstrator, the trainer asks, "What are your takeaways from this?" The demonstrator gets the final word and sets her own course for next steps.

SCHOOL IMPLEMENTATIONS

When a school decides to implement VTS across all classes and all grades, which is the way to ensure equal access for all students as well as the maximum chance of the sequential benefits of VTS to take hold, the professional development plan calls for daylong introductory workshops at the beginning of each year for three years and a series of debriefings spaced between opportunities to teach the ten lessons— usually between three and five sessions each of the three years the lessons are phased in. These might be scheduled after school, before school, or during in-service days, depending on the particular school.

The content of the debriefings ranges from brainstorming solutions to problems encountered during lessons—kids who dominate, for example, or ones who hold back—to exercises having to do with VTS elements such as paraphrasing or linking.

Many kinds of questions come up. Once participants get over the initial satisfaction of seeing many kids engage in VTS, for example, skepticism about what it accomplishes is almost inevitable, particularly given a context dominated by direct instruction. VTS is in fact another teaching paradigm, complementary to be sure, but still different enough to take time to digest why and how it works. Explanations help, but the real validation of VTS emerges over time and even then only if reflected upon.

After a few lessons, therefore, it's legitimate to rethink, "Now why is it that I let mistakes pass by?" Or, "What would it hurt if I added information?" Or, "Why no other questions, particularly when I think the students are on to something I can help direct?" Or, "Is this more than fun for the kids?" These and other quandaries get brought up, quite legitimately, during both coaching and debriefings, and one reason for spreading VTS training over time is because answers puzzled through by groups of teachers are deeper as experience accumulates.

As part of the training, teachers are also mentored twice a year when a trainer comes to visit each classroom for coteaching and one-on-one coaching: both trainer and teacher facilitate one or two discussions, and each has a chance to observe the other. Importantly, both also get to see the students in operation, usually a treat for the teacher especially. Short minicoaching takes place immediately afterward, so both coach and teacher can think through what they just saw as well as providing feedback and thoughts about what to work on.

The VTS organization provides an online means to reflect after each lesson by way of a series of questions timed to coordinate with what experience has told us are issues at given points in time. Teachers can post their thoughts and thereby keep a record of how the process evolves. The Web site also provides networking opportunities and links to other teachers who are implementing VTS.

The Web site contains a large compendium of information, including answers to a set of frequently asked questions. All of the research reports are posted. Voluntary online seminars and roundtables bring together VTS practitioners from all over to hear each other's ideas and experience. VTS trainers are available for thoughts and questions by way of e-mail.

IN SUMMARY

Understanding VTS happens most efficiently when answers to questions result from exchange among peers. VTS professional development provides a structure for this, enabling teachers to talk themselves into understanding the rationale behind the method as well as the learning nurtured over time, just as students talk themselves into new uses of language and thinking processes over the course of repeated image discussions. And that's the point of the training we evolved over twenty years: to give teachers the opportunity to use what they already know to understand what might seem challenging about VTS.

Learning to use VTS and, further, to believe in its efficacy, is a matter of pulling back from the classroom experience to consider what both we and the kids are learning. Learning VTS virtually turns us into field researchers—watching students, noting and analyzing behaviors, and thinking about the implications—as it has for Marion Bageant, Craig Madison, and others.

What enables these teachers to examine the behaviors of their students productively is the fact that they do VTS well. They maximize its potential. Rachel Zender, the sixth-grade teacher introduced earlier, speaks convincingly about how a teacher's command of VTS affects student behavior. She includes listening as a required skill, and comments on how this can be "hard in part because teachers usually have to have their minds on what's next, but they have to be present to make VTS work. Memorizing questions made it easier for me to listen. And once I found myself really listening, I was much more sensitive to both their language and eventually my own as I paraphrased."

Linda Sugano teaches fourth grade in Spokane. She's taught for over thirty years, ten of those in bilingual education. She thinks of teaching and student behavior as intimately intertwined in another way: as she repeats the second VTS question (asking for evidence) in order for students to pick up the habit, she, too, builds a habit and finds herself working the questions into other teaching. It's easy to fold into math lessons because the curriculum her school uses also emphasizes evidence, and while not directly using VTS in that context, the familiar VTS phrasing of the question helps her students go deeper with their thinking.

Linda also comments that becoming adept at paraphrasing provides the students with an example of reflecting on what one takes in, something that she wants them to do and that is also sought by Common Core standards: the habit of showing you understand, something demonstrated by paraphrasing. She has found that the constancy of paraphrasing throughout the VTS professional development at her school has produced new levels of respect for one another as teachers clarify what they have to say. This has a positive impact on teacher interactions, but she also cites a student who had basically given up on himself (we're talking about a nine-year-old) who seems to have found some self-respect through VTS: his ideas are validated by Linda as she paraphrases, by other students as they appreciate that he's made observations no one else has thought of, and by their own responses to his comments. Linda has seen his behavior change in other classes.

These teachers basically echo the sentiments I have come to over many years and multiple trainings: a teacher can begin to use VTS quickly, but getting good at it takes time and is greatly aided by help from others, especially fellow teachers—one's peers. Practicing it well opens enormous potential for helping students, but it also leads to teacher growth: the possibility of really understanding thinking, of having much deeper insights into one's students, of digging more deeply into what makes language occur and how to help all students reach their potential.

Take some time to think about this. In the end, it's not my thoughts that matter. It's yours. I'm describing what I've come to know over time by reflecting on experiences I've had, and I've spent a lot of time with VTS. I've made valuable discoveries along the way, and the purpose of this book is to share them, as much as possible through the words of experienced classroom teachers. That said, we only "sort of" learn from what we read or hear from others; to learn in a way that sticks with us, we have to actively take in those examples and ideas, engage with them in our own practice, sift them through our own filters, and find our own examples and words to explain them before we even know if they are useful to us. You know I could go on describing myriad justifications and insights related to VTS, but I want your stance always to be skeptical: he believes this, but what makes it useful to me? Does it work for me? Is it true, or true for me? If I think it might be so, how might I put it into my words? How would I explain it to others?

If, over the course of your thinking about VTS, your deliberations add up to thinking that it works as it's prescribed, you're more likely to try applying it, with the necessary adjustments, to other subjects as the teachers described in this book do. And you will also be more inclined to consider what an analysis of thinking found in writing samples might add to the assessment strategies you use. And you'll have a leg up on meeting Common Core standards.

CHAPTER 7

Effective Teaching

IT IS MY DEEPLY HELD conviction that both teachers and students are capable of much higher levels of performance than the current system allows or measures—and you as teachers know this. I believe that performance-based reviews of teachers will in time include fairer, richer, and more comprehensive measures than scores on standardized tests and that good teaching will once again incorporate more than rigorously adhering to mandated curricula. I believe that all of us can be effective, achieving high-level performance from kids who currently falter as well as those who are capable of shining but don't.

VTS provides a window into how to switch the emphasis from "effective teachers" to "effective teaching," something I hope might help many who are, in fact, good teachers but who operate against unmanageable odds out of their control—the debilitating impact of poverty, for example. Once the facilitation process becomes second nature to teachers, they can apply VTS in many lessons, calling into play students' skills in thinking and group communication that stem from the annual ten image lessons. Particularly when so applied, VTS abets direct instruction, addresses many standards stressed by those in control of education funding and policy, and provides tools to help students deal with questions requiring comprehension and evidence. VTS will offer a bigger boost when Common Core testing augments or replaces existing forms. But its impact is not limited to these markers of achievement.

All the teachers cited in this book believe that VTS has helped them become more effective in achieving what they have always believed in: helping kids become their best possible selves. They were all exemplary teachers already; with this additional tool they have expanded their reach to kids marginalized by the narrow focus of required instruction and standardized tests either because they were behind to begin with or because they are held back by the lack of stimulating challenges.

The point of this chapter is to help teachers arm themselves to ar-gue for changes in—or at least additions to—the dominant practices in instruction. I hope many of us work together to expand the denomina-tors of achievement to allow more teachers and more kids to excel.

Earlier in this book, I tried to provide insight into the cognitive research bases of VTS in an attempt to explain the behaviors we see resulting from it. In this chapter, I want to set VTS in the context of a particular understanding of pedagogy well argued by distinguished thinkers such as John Dewey and Jerome Bruner and that passes the acid test of common sense as well: learning happens within the learner; others only help.

HOW DID WE GET TO WHERE WE ARE?

When I was in elementary school around the cusp of 1950, we read Dick and Jane aloud in class, and schoolbooks on various subjects were passed along year after year. Teachers decided how well we wrote and read along with how accurately we added, subtracted, and eventually did our multiplication tables, aided by answers in the teachers' editions of our texts. In order to fill out report cards, they applied a general sense of what was appropriate. Academic performance was not all teachers commented upon; we were also marked for citizenship—a euphemism for behavior—and we knew our parents would be told if we weren't "working up to our potential" or if we caused trouble.

It might have been different for kids who lived in urban centers instead of the midwestern town where we lived, but as far as I can remember, most young people shared expectations of themselves and of those around them. We did what was expected of us in school and at home—at least most of the time. And I don't recall that it was ever the teacher's fault when we didn't.

This mid-twentieth-century system managed to prepare most of us for later education, including college, and also for the jobs that were waiting. That said—and this is a serious qualification—coping with the vast changes of the ensuing decades hasn't been easy for my generation, and facing up to challenges such as pollution and climate change has been too slow.

In his 1970 book, *Future Shock*, Alvin Toffler parsed the education model I just described as having been adequate for the industrial society—schools preparing people for factories with routines, bells, and tasks—but wholly ill-suited to changing technology and other innovation, phenomena that have escalated in the forty years since.[1] In one statement attributed to him, Toffler says, "The illiterate of the 21st Century will not be those who cannot read and write, but those who cannot learn, unlearn, and relearn."

Perhaps because this is only half true (reading and writing remain essential abilities of successful people today), it was hard for educators to know how to address the other, "true" part—the need to teach people to be comfortable with adapting to changes in information and opportunity. Knowing how to shift gears and accommodate new circumstances requires more than the command of certain skills and a body of knowledge: we have to know how to learn.

Toffler helped instigate a lot of talk about reforming and reshaping education, and even some consensus that change was needed, but he provided no strategies to help make it happen. Even less radical critics with proposals for new approaches had little impact on the system at large. Whatever solutions were put forward failed to catch on for many reasons: unproven effectiveness on a large scale, the difficulty in taking something that worked in one environment into new ones, the challenge of scaling up to the point where good ideas could be widely tried, and a lack of clarity about how to improve practice and no consensus as to what was needed. Teaching conventions basically stayed in place and discrepancies in performance gradually worsened. Both colleges and employers more and more often deplored the lack of preparedness for advanced study and for the kinds of work available.

Concern built over the course of the 1980s, inspired in part by the 1983 report *A Nation at Risk*, commissioned by President Ronald Reagan's Secretary of Education. The risk it described addressed more the quality of education than equality of opportunity, though it asserted the right of all to a great education.

The study's focus was the decreasing abilities of American students compared to other nations in the developed world. Here are the first lines of the summary: "Our Nation is at risk. Our once unchallenged preeminence in commerce, industry, science, and technological innovation is being overtaken by competitors throughout the world."[2] The report harshly judged the quality of secondary education in particular. That was thirty years ago, but similar perceptions continue to make headlines today.

The drive for standards is predicated on values most of us share: the need to provide, through elementary and secondary schooling, equal opportunity for all young people to find success in later life. Despite the desire for equity and steps taken to achieve it, however, statistics over several decades continue to show uneven impact across demographic groups. Although the factors that make it so are many and complicated, economic deprivation is a consistent determinant. Kids who live in poverty come to school unprepared for achievement in too many subjects and particularly struggle with the pace of academic demands. The huge numbers of students who don't know English or speak it at home is a factor; an assistant superintendent in a Texas city said to me that "our kids are illiterate in two languages." Parents with limited educations themselves are unable to help their children with schoolwork. Frequent administrative turnover, inconsistent leadership, funding cutbacks, harsh criticism, and the resultant low morale are also elements.

The push for fairness across demographics is necessary. Teachers, perhaps even more than others, want to set up all young people to succeed throughout their lives in school and want their educations to enable them to meet the demands of tomorrow's workplace. Still, standardization of curricula is a challenge when the playing field isn't level; uniformity of approach is not a solution to multifaceted problems. Many teachers, perhaps most, have therefore found it hard to bring their students to performance levels realistic only for some but unreasonable for others. Some standards are improbable goals to begin with—the amount of material that is supposed to be covered, for example, and lack of consideration of developmental readiness—but even ones that make sense in terms of time, available resources, and development are hard to meet with students who are drastically behind when they come to school.

When statewide testing became common in the late 1990s, the statistics revealed a picture that could not be ignored. The problem surfaces in shameful graduation rates, especially in cities, and the inconsistency of achievement across a broad spectrum of schools—discrepancies between schools serving affluent and middle-class students and those serving poor, often minority students. While statistics in the last few years indicate some forward movement in helping those who struggle, far too many still fail or make it through lacking many basic competencies.

This has ramifications. For example, in December 2010, the Education Trust reported that "the first-ever public analysis of data from the Army's Armed Services Vocational Aptitude Battery (ASVAB), the test that determines if applicants qualify to enlist in the military" concluded that "too few of our nation's recent high school graduates—particularly young people of color—have the math, reading, science, and problem-solving skills necessary for enlistment in the U.S. Army."[3] According to the report, 23 percent of recent high school graduates didn't get the minimum score needed to enlist in any military branch, and it was considerably worse for students of color. If unprepared to enter the military, who's ready for research or new technology jobs?

Political interest in public school performance has waxed and waned over the years, but lawmakers turned the spotlight on achievement in part as a result of the civil rights movements beginning in the 1930s. As public opinion and, finally in 1954, the courts decided that segregated schools were never equal; as middle-class people fled the cities for the suburbs; and as cities became poorer and increasingly dominated by the poor and immigrant populations, the issue of maintaining fair, effective, and equal educations for all young people contributed to a politicization of schooling such as we see today.

The performance gap reflects societal flaws, nothing inherent in the kids. Many parents of poor children grew up in poverty themselves, often in other countries, and their own educations are spotty and academic skills low. They can't prepare their children to come to school ready to play the game as we did. Compounded by a lack of time to help their children and few resources ubiquitous in homes like the one I grew up in—books, for example—parents enroll kids in schools unaware of their lack of preparation. Wyla's kindergarten teacher told me that the homework assigned was mostly to teach parents what is taught in school since many didn't know. These children are not in fact ready to start where lessons begin and are sometimes confused by sitting in rows, opening their books, and engaging as my classmates and I did. Poverty produces some cognitive damage too, but part of what puts disadvantaged children at risk of failure is that they are not primed for what school asks of them. I was just told of a New York City kindergarten teacher whose students are expected to write five-sentence paragraphs. The pool of five-year-olds able to succeed at this task is pretty small.

As a society, we've done little to offset the disadvantages caused by poverty. We have only to look at the scarcity of early-childhood care and education centers to see how little priority we place on rectifying a situation thoughtful people have known to exist for decades. Programs like Head Start serve roughly 20 percent of the children up to age five who live in poverty in California, for example, according to First 5

California, a state-funded watchdog that maintains a profile on children in the state; its figures jibe with those supplied by Head Start itself across the nation. And funding is being reduced further as I write, so the number of children given this boost will diminish further.

The problems are a public concern at this point, though how visibly depends almost on the year. It's no secret that most educational and social service budgets have been slashed since the recession began in 2008, and the process hasn't ended. It's been worsened by the sequester of 2013. But even before recent cuts, solutions to challenges were typically taking the form of standards, standardization of curricula, and testing rather than real changes to the ways teachers get to teach.

Here's one pretty bleak way to look at this: school finances have seldom been more compromised, too many kids don't make proficiency in subjects where the standards aren't that high anyway, bright kids aren't challenged, teachers are being blamed for lack of achievement, social conditions that underlie failure only get worse, too few school leaders actually help, and morale is in the toilet. Schools and teachers are supposed to do triage on damage beyond their skill sets and resources. Solutions to education's problems are imposed by entities that seem out of touch, sensible criticisms of these solutions are ignored, and teachers have almost no voice. And the same entities feel they can judge the performances of teachers. We have been dealt a lousy hand. So what to do given a tough situation? Get tough ourselves. What do we have to lose by taking on the problem ourselves, classroom by classroom, school by school? Buoyed by standards that actually inspire, can we collectively turn this challenging time into the opportunity to achieve what we all want?

CONSTRUCTING KNOWLEDGE

Looking and wondering is a powerful process. As we see each day with the young ones in our lives, childhood curiosity is unbounded and almost unstoppable. The integration of observing and language development is one of the most remarkable human capabilities. By the time they are school age, most children are wired to use their acute sensory perceptions, paired with language, to learn.

This set of miracles happens, beginning in infancy, without formal teaching and progresses for the most part naturally. Conscientious parents and other adults significantly aid the process by introducing experiences and opportunities, talking to their charges and naming what comes to the child's attention, but children are the agents of their learning. They teach themselves to walk and talk, to feed themselves, to use scissors and paint, to read and spell. We help only by providing examples, creating the chance to learn, and interacting with them as they explore. We assist in necessary ways, but they do the work.

Ironically, the remarkable cognition of which children are capable is almost taken for granted, and the fact of children's essential role in learning is little recognized either at home or at school. By the time kids are three, four, and five, both teachers and parents spend a lot of time telling them what to do, wear, eat, and learn. Adults read to young ones, quickly turning pages to follow the course of the written text and making only cursory reference to illustrations. Preschool and kindergarten—once places of open-ended exploration of many resources, play, art making, and time for supervised but undirected activity—are now heavily structured with tasks that emphasize behavioral rules, letters and words, and numbers and counting, virtually all of it teacher-directed.

We know why this happens: we have to get them reading; we're readying them for tests that loom. But concentration on memorizing doesn't capitalize on the visual acuity of children, give them the chance to figure out stories using their eye/mind connections, or find their own words to tell the stories—a fluency that, to my way of thinking, aids the learning-to-read process more than the supposed fast-tracking that comes from direct instruction.

With their brains already working in wonderfully complicated ways, think about how to capitalize on the instinctual processes of very young children.

- How can we help young ones maintain their ability and interest in observing, and in time help them direct their gaze, not simply follow their noses?
- How can we help them sort out, reflect on, and use what they see?
- Can we make them aware that this natural instinct of theirs is a strategy they can apply consciously to learn?
- What can we do to guide them to use these skills to develop others?

There are obvious answers to these questions:

- Keep them looking.
- And ask them to talk about what they see.

In other words, continue to exercise a circuit of seeing, listening, and talking, natural operations that seem to go underground when children are regimented. Whether looking carefully at pictures or observing a phenomenon in nature—plants sprouting, changing shapes of the moon, ants scurrying along the pavement—build on children's strengths to help them see even more. Encourage them to talk about what interests them, building both language and thinking skills. Gradually use that amassing of ability as the foundation and springboard for reading and math. As a sixth-grade student of my colleague, Carol Henderson, summarized the image discussion process, "At first you wonder, what the heck is this? And then after talking for a while your brain gets a boost and you have an idea."

Acknowledgment that we learn through experience is as old as humans, I suspect. Think of skills and knowledge passed along by older generations to their children through the age-old process of apprenticeship, something still effectively used in medical education and architecture. You learn from doing, applying, and practicing the craft, guided by masters and referring to sources of information when you need them.

The matter of one generation teaching another by way of demonstration and doing, abetted by bits of advice here and there, goes well beyond professional training. In the past, we learned to sow, sew, cook, nurture, tend the healthy and the ill—on and on—by full circles of activity from watching or being shown to naming, trying, practicing, repeating, adding, and changing. We learned about time from observing nature close at hand, conventions from following examples, the past from stories told to us by elders, and essential beliefs from observing and participating in rituals. We learned how to solve problems through guided practice of many chores and life experiences.

Society has changed and with that we live further from nature, without the need to work the way we once did, and often without the close contact of earlier generations who shared, un-self-consciously, their knowledge and insights. Families now typically hand over a great deal of teaching to schools and professionals assigned the tasks of helping students learn what they need to know as established by society, regardless of its perceived relevance to the kids themselves.

What hasn't changed is the human learner. Inspired by Confucius, influential thinker John Dewey formulated valuable theory around a particular notion of how we learn. It has come to be known as *constructivism*: the notion that we construct our understandings of things over time by self-directed activity.

Most schooling these days involves doing, albeit in a limited sphere. Testing has reduced the curricula of many schools to little more than reading, writing, and math, and asking teachers to teach the required tasks mostly through demonstrations, explanations, and repetitive exercises. Huge amounts of time are assigned to direct instruction in prioritized subjects while teachers squeeze other subjects in the margins.

But statistics tell us that many kids don't learn and/or don't retain what they seem to take in. Why?

One set of reasons, I believe, has to do with what we realized at MOMA: our teaching was out of sync with the developmental levels of our visitors. Individuals can learn only what they are prepared to assimilate and eventually accommodate, as early developmentalist Jean Piaget put it, and can learn only what is within reach at a given moment—what Lev Vygotsky called the "zone of proximal development." Like the pedals of a tricycle: until their legs stretch that far, a child can't make the wheels turn.

I have over forty years' experience in education—teaching, designing, and running programs; observing classrooms across the country; and doing a lot of reading and thinking—and I have come to the conclusion that many requirements of education today are out of line with what kids are ready to learn, and ignore the uneven preparedness of students as they enter school. As a result, I believe it would be smart to adjust our sense of timing: rethink when desired skills or the acquisition of certain knowledge should be stressed.

Developmental data exists to help guide this, and can be consulted for realistic instruction and expectations of achievement. The Gesell Institute has years of data about thresholds in early childhood learning—what to expect when. One of the Institute's cornerstone beliefs is that we cannot expect children to perform tasks according to schedules they are not ready for. It won't happen. Brains are not wired to accommodate unreasonable expectations.[4]

In addition to developmental parameters, another reason for limited achievement has to do with intrinsic motivation, or perhaps more accurately, the lack of it. Children who have not been read to might be confused by the emphasis on reading that begins in preschool and is doubled down on in kindergarten. They could easily lack a personal connection to much of what they are expected to learn. It's not hard to see that those who are well prepared and supported by assistance at home achieve more quickly than those who are not.

The challenges to meeting learning demands are widespread. The Bill and Melinda Gates Foundation Web site[5] posts this distressing message prominently in its section on early childhood:

> To get off to the right start, children need to enter kindergarten emotionally, socially, and intellectually ready for learning. If they are unprepared in these ways and lack other early skills—such as knowing colors, sitting still, following directions, or getting along with others—they may start kindergarten behind and never catch up. Experts estimate that more than half the children in Washington State enter kindergarten without the skills they need to succeed.

This is not hyperbole and Washington State is not unique. If a child doesn't know colors, think of the other vocabulary that's missing—vocabulary, even a sense of words and their purpose, that is essential for a child to be ready to read. And when she doesn't know how to follow directions or sit still, what makes anyone think she is prepared to focus, memorize letters, and learn phonetics? Still, standards and curricula for early childhood education in our test-driven educational culture push reading in ways that could be counterproductive even with kids who are supposedly ready. When children still need to be learning from play, we're busy accentuating academic skill.

And what happens when we push a child to learn something that remains "unlearned"? One distinct possibility is that he learns he can fail. Because of being unready—no fault of his—he fails at the alphabet, and if discouragement begins to set in, we have compounded an already challenging problem. It's not hard to see in kindergartens and first grades: the kids who already know that they are not measuring up. I've watched Eduardo at Wyla's school for the past two years, and he's pretty beaten down. It's not his brain that's problematic. It's what's expected of him. I am convinced that were he taught differently, in a manner more inclusive of both his needs and his potential, it would be different.

Why do we make this mistake? Why don't we instead capitalize on what even those who operate from disadvantage are already good at to gradually build toward other learning? Think back again to Wyla: she learned the word *alligator* not because anyone put it on a spelling list, but because she wanted to. It was relevant. Learning is not just a matter of rote "doing" but also, gradually and incrementally, incorporating what is useful. Even if he comes to school disadvantaged by comparison, we could make it up to Eduardo if we taught differently. Marion Bageant is doing this with Allen, her "Eduardo," and it's working. Remember, he got a near-perfect score on the later math unit tests. Her other highly challenged student achieves similarly.

If I were inventing the instruction to reach the standards put forward by Common Core and prepare young people to meet the challenges of our ever-more-complicated, global, rapidly changing world, I would structure learning environments to:

- Let the content of our teaching emerge from meaningful and expanded encounters with the real world; this is what engages kids: finding meaning in and negotiating the lives they lead.
- Concentrate on developing skills that enable students to explore and interact with others and their environment in ways that are meaningful to them.
- Enlarge the notion of necessary literacies in the way that Common Core standards outline: speaking, listening, communicating, knowing how to direct their learning in all content areas, and decoding diverse material.
- Remain developmentally appropriate: always give learners tasks and challenges that are within reach.
- Build in peer learning—authentic collaboration in problem solving.
- Nurture young people as we introduce information and discipline; help them know they are smart and capable.

From this list of recommendations, it will be apparent that effective teaching would consist almost entirely of creating a structure or environment for learning. The real work is the active, creative accomplishment of the student with help from others. This is one way of describing what Marion, Craig, Tracy, and others are doing: helping their students learn. They have decided they can do this in part by applying VTS— and its constructivist basis—to other lessons.

To find the will to change, we have to examine our values, what we hold true. Let's think for a moment of the values that are at the core of believing that people construct their own knowledge and skills. We need to believe that children naturally want to learn and to succeed and are capable of doing it, even without direct instruction. We need to think that, when motivated by interest, children are capable of self-discipline and will undertake work with as much enthusiasm as they do play and seek opportunity on their own initiative. We need to remember that they learn only by doing, with "doing" understood to include thinking and speaking alongside more traditional activity. We need to respect them as individuals at all ages, allowing them to make choices among reasonable options and responsible decisions with guidance. We give them a chance to learn from each other and trust that they will turn to adults for assistance and support when needed. We need to recognize that they will respond to feedback, including criticism, when it's dealt fairly and evenly.

My experience as a parent, grandparent, teacher, researcher, and study junkie tell me that these reflect reasonable assessments of children's natural behavior—true even for many kids born with disabilities. While I suspect many parents and educators agree with some of these assessments, both at home and at school, we organize, schedule, assign, correct, referee, and limit to such an extent that we as a culture don't know what would happen if we didn't. Even the debilitations of poverty and learning challenges don't change the potential in each young person; they simply complicate the timing of achievement and call for different strategies for teaching and remediating.

Think about this. Does it make sense to you?

A CHALLENGE

In the summer of 2010, Common Core, the effort spearheaded by a consortium of governors, published standards that are on their way to becoming national. Their point is to equalize expectations and performance across the United States and also to set objectives that more directly address twenty-first-century needs—more the kind of schooling suggested by Alvin Toffler. Relevant tests are being developed.

Teachers in this book show that a small shift in strategies can ameliorate and even solve knotty problems presented by learning-disabled kids, ones debilitated by poverty, or ones coping with the need to achieve in a language they've just begun to learn when faced with unaccommodating and not-always-interesting curricula. Using the same basic strategy, some of these teachers have recharged able kids, giving them insights and experience they translate into thoughtful, artful writing: young people poised to grow more. Some of this sampling of teachers have added questions, activities, and assessment schema, all in a constructivist mode, and from the looks of it the resultant learning is authentic. These teachers are conscientious, exemplary, altogether admirable, and likeable, but they aren't superhuman. They are busy mortals like you and me, who for a variety of reasons, have decided to address at least some of their teaching dilemmas and opportunities in a new way, guided by VTS.

I'm making a pitch here. Common Core standards, more than any we've seen to date, urge us to recreate instruction to serve the real needs of young people and, if we're successful, give them tools to succeed in education and work. The intended achievement is inspiring; it addresses both timeworn priorities and new ones that stress thinking, a wider range of literacies, oral expression, listening—skills needed across disciplinary boundaries. The skills outlined by Common Core standards position young people not just to get through school but to thrive in a world that requires a broad set of competencies, primary among them the capacity to grasp unfamiliar material, define new problems, and find innovative solutions—and to do it collaboratively.

Wisely, the authors of Common Core leave it up to teachers to design the means to reach the new objectives. What has happened in the past when new educational goals are set, and what will very likely happen again, however, is that publishers seize the new marketing opportunity and create curricula as well as assessment measures to fill the need. The results of their efforts—you know the curricula; you've doubtless moved through several generations—are seldom what is promised. Couldn't teachers drive an alternative means of meeting this new challenge?

We have a moment when neither Common Core nor the powerful school publishing community has determined how to teach or measure the new skill sets. If teachers decided to do their own exploring and course creation by working together—and "together" these days, given social media, means that the collective of teacher voices can be widespread—I'm convinced that teacher-formed curricula could influence the direction of where things go.

I wrote this book super-conscious of the pressures on teachers today. Basic VTS involves only ten lessons both because that's enough to produce significant growth, and importantly, because we want to take as little class time as possible. Applications of it in language arts and math involve little or no extra time, fitting easily within blocks of time set aside for these subjects. They demand little extracurricular time planning.

But that isn't true of the most adventurous applications—Craig and El Verano's indigenously designed curricula, Brian's social studies classes, Carol's "image a day," and Tracy's "poem a day." These take time and effort outside of class as well as blocks of time within. They are best accomplished with teams of teachers focusing together on the objectives appropriate for their students and the teaching strategies designed to meet those objectives. That said, I hope I've made the case for the worth of efforts like those of the teachers described herein: the lessons simultaneously build thinking and language skills authentically, engagingly introduce concepts and content in other subjects that are hard to teach, and directly advance the challenges of Common Core.

The assessment model I described in chapter 4 (and again in the appendix) might also be part of what teachers introduce to the process of adopting Common Core. It, too, requires extra time from teachers as they learn to analyze writing samples for thinking content as well as for verbal expression. It also requires time collecting, keeping, and meeting with the students. But in my view (you won't be surprised to read), the time is well spent both for the teacher who develops new analytical skills and an enriched understanding of thinking as well as for what it could mean to students. Helping students become aware of their thinking, as it appears hand-in-hand with written expression, and providing tools for rethinking, adding, and editing as a integral activity, not an exercise, directly assists the meeting of the Common Core skills for college and work readiness. When and if such a practice becomes natural for you, you will have concrete evidence of real change to help you introduce this method of qualitative assessment to others who normally seek quantitative measures. At this point, it's still just an idea, but it conforms to another new movement, assessment *for* learning, designed to help students directly benefit from assessment—a paradigm shift from the more typical assessment *of* learning.

PERMISSION TO WONDER

We're in the midst of an important change, and its direction shouldn't simply be accepted without scrutiny. Be skeptical of Common Core. Be skeptical of all that I've written. Apply that same questioning lens to what you see going on in your own classrooms now. Think about what is required of you and your students by direct instruction, and weigh the merits: whom it serves well, whom it doesn't. Figure out which of the standards are sensible, which are not, and what goals and objectives you would establish instead in different subjects for the students you teach. Think about the challenges and delights posed by the range of the students you face every day. Think about what steps you want to take to improve the likelihood that all—the most challenged, the most difficult, the most gifted—become all they can be. Examine the Common Core standards with your peers to make sure you understand and agree with the directions; temper them with your knowledge and experience.

Among the lessons VTS has taught us is that we nurture achievement most when we start any teaching/learning process by asking students to do something already possible, ideally familiar and natural, and perceived as valuable by learners: interesting to them. The fact of them using their eyes to figure out what's going on around them, the way they listen to what people say to pick up language, the interest they have in making sense of what they see and hear—each of these provides a strong starting point for teaching that sticks, expanding and extending a child's abilities.

If you (hopefully with your fellow teachers) begin to observe VTS in action—first with art, then with other subjects—you're bound to come up with new discoveries and untried ideas. And while I want to leave you with the notion that VTS can bring joy along with substantial learning to your kids' lives, I want you to know that we constantly learn from wondering about it and its impact. Such wondering is what will make meeting new standards a rewarding challenge for you and your kids. That's worth remembering.

APPENDIX

If You're Interested in Trying VTS

CHAPTER 1: PERMISSION TO WONDER

Teachers can learn more about the rationale and purpose behind VTS by reading the research that was used to study viewing skills and to construct a method for examining and discussing images. Abigail Housen describes her research protocol and the theory of aesthetic development that resulted from her years of study in a series of articles available on the VTS Web site: http://vtshome.org/research. Research conducted over twelve years of VTS field work, including the impact of VTS on student thinking, is described in reports also posted there. There are two multiyear studies and many smaller ones, all at least summarized on the Web site.

The same URL will give you access to independent studies that have addressed VTS's impact on thinking and related performance. One of these, a three-year study completed in 2005 called the Artful Citizenship Project, was funded by the U.S. Department of Education (DOE) and developed in partnership with The Wolfsonian-FIU and the Miami-Dade County Public Schools. The Project undertook to understand the relationship between visual literacy and academic and social skills. Some of its findings were that at the end of three years there was a strong relationship between growth in visual literacy and growth in both reading and mathematics; VTS promoted cooperation, respect, and tolerance for the views of others; and VTS was especially effective with students with limited English proficiency. These behaviors were not found in control students. The study concluded that curriculum enhancements like VTS may be the best test preparation schools can provide.

Another study was conducted by the Isabella Stewart Gardner Museum in partnership with the Institute for Learning Innovation. Completed in 2007, the study was also funded by a three-year grant from the federal DOE to research students' learning from the Gardner Museum's multiple-visit VTS program. It concluded that students in the program, compared to control students, generated significantly more instances of various aspects of critical thinking, had more to say, and were more likely to provide evidence to back up their thinking.

Project Zero, a part of Harvard's Graduate School of Education, conducted a study of an early draft of VTS, then called the Visual Thinking Curriculum (VTC), in New York City schools. According to the Project Zero Web site:

Highlights of the major research findings are:

- The VTC tends to contribute to a modest but statistically significant increase in the quality of students' evidential reasoning when they are forming interpretations about the meaning of a work of art. This gain also appears to transfer to forming interpretations about the meaning of a non-art image in the domain of science.
- The VTC tends to contribute to a modest but significant increase in students' awareness of the subjective, or conditional, nature of interpretation. Like the gains in evidential reasoning, this is a gain in the context of interpreting the meaning of a work of art, and also in the context of interpreting the meaning of a non-art image in the domain of science.

- In the area of evidential reasoning, the gains that students make as a result of the VTC do not appear limited to students of high ability or low ability. Most students experience at least modest gains, and the gains do not appear to favor students of a particular ability level.

A longer summary is available at http://www.pz.gse.harvard.edu/moma.php.

CHAPTER 2: VISUAL THINKING STRATEGIES: THE BASICS

Teachers usually find it beneficial to seek training in VTS facilitation. Information about training can be found for schools at http://vtshome .org/training--2/for-schools, and for individuals at http://vtshome.org/ training--2/for-individuals. The basic steps for conducting a VTS discussion are as follows:

1. Present a carefully selected image, based on Housen/VTS research criteria. Ideal images contain:
   - Subjects of interest given the specific audience
   - Familiar imagery given audience
   - Strong narratives
   - Accessible meanings given audience
   - Ambiguity: complex enough to puzzle

2. Allow a few moments for silent looking before beginning the discussion.

3. Pose three specific research-tested questions to motivate and maintain the inquiry:
   - What's going on/happening in this picture?
   - What do you see that makes you say that?
   - What more can you/we find?

4. Facilitate the discussion by:
   - Listening carefully to catch all students say
   - Pointing to observations as students comment, a "visual paraphrase"
   - Paraphrasing each comment, taking a moment to reflect on it while formulating the response to make sure all content and meanings are grasped and helpfully rephrased
   - Linking related comments whether students agree or disagree, or build on one another's ideas
   - Remaining neutral by treating everyone and each comment in the same way
   - Concluding by thanking students for their participation

In schools that implement VTS, one-hour, image-based discussions are conducted ten times a year beginning in kindergarten. Images used are sequenced so that students discuss more challenging images over time and are exposed to a diversity of media and images representing different styles and periods. Lesson plans, images, and a huge compendium of information about VTS to aid in implementation are available at a subscription Web site; this URL provides information about how to subscribe: http://vtsweb.org/vts-subscriptions.

CHAPTER 3: APPLYING VTS TO OTHER SUBJECTS

VTS begins with discussion of art; once students learn relevant thinking and social behaviors, the method can be applied to other subjects. When applying VTS to text, math, social studies, and science lessons, for example, teachers use the same steps and methods used for discussions of art images described in chapter 2. However, the questions are adapted slightly based on the type of subject under discussion; the following suggestions are not research-based as VTS questions are, but based on observations of teachers at work.

Questions for text:

- What's going on in this poem/story/text? (Or more simply: What's going on here?)
- What did you read, or what words did you read, that make you say that?
- What more can you find?

Questions for math:

- What's going on here, or with this problem? (Or: What does this problem ask us to do/find out?)
- What did you read/see that makes you think that?
- What more can you find?
- How might we solve this problem?
- What did you read/see that makes you think that?
- Are there other possibilities?

Questions for other imagery (such as scientific or historical photos):

- Begin with the standard VTS questions but follow-up questions are usually appropriate as well.
- What do you know about [fossils, for example, or shadows]?
- What can we learn from this [letter, chart, map, or diagram]?
- What more are you curious to know?
- How might we find the answer to that question?
- How might we find out if we're correct?
- What else might we want to find out?
- How might we do that?

Many such discussions open up a topic and either individual, pair, or group projects follow, often based on questions or subjects the students themselves identify. Such follow-up depends on the subject and the intent of the lesson, and gives both teachers and students room to be inventive as well as directive in their inquiries.

CHAPTER 4: ASSESSING THINKING THROUGH WRITING

As student thinking skills become an important aspect of standards, it's germane to develop ways to understand and appreciate them. The ephemeral nature of discussions is one reason we recommend collecting writing samples to chart the growth and development in students as a result of VTS. These samples provide concrete evidence of change. To do this, collect one sample from all students before beginning VTS any given year, using the following prompts, and then a second at the end of the year. If you use the same picture both times, comparisons between before and after are clearer.

> *Look closely at this image. Think carefully about what you see. Ask yourself:*
>
> - *What's going on in this picture?*
> - *What do I see that makes me say that?*
> - *What more can I find?*
>
> *You have 15 to 20 minutes to write. Try to organize your writing to make it easy for others to understand your thoughts. Be sure to read over your work and make corrections to your writing.*

Images and forms for collecting writing samples are available on the VTS Web site created for teachers and available by subscription: http://vtsweb.org/vts-subscriptions. Examples of student writing are available at the VTS public Web site: http://vtshome.org/research.

To add to the "before and after" samples, give students a chance to write after at least some of the discussions and keep these samples as well. This means that you and the student both have a record of his thinking as a result of the group process, often more developed than what he might do alone. You can review all the samples collected at the end of the year.

The thinking that you want to monitor can be categorized as follows:

- Observations: likely to go from few and simple to more detailed and elaborated
- Inferences: meanings drawn from the observations
- Evidence: pinpointing observations to back up inferences, often expressed as some form of "I think this because," though equally often simply implied
- Speculation: considering multiple options, usually expressed with qualifying language such as "could or might be" and providing optional interpretations
- Elaboration: returning to a topic to add detail
- Revision: some form of "At first I thought . . . but then I thought . . ."

Once VTS practice becomes second nature to you—and it usually takes a while—both paraphrasing and linking serve as tools for knowing how students are thinking. For the moments you are considering how to paraphrase a comment and how it might connect to others, you are, in a way, inside a child's head, reflecting on bits of data, considering what he notices and how he interprets it. Although it isn't easy, it's possible—especially if you make a few notes after class—to reflect on what you hear and compare it to what you expected or to what you have heard in earlier conversations.

All that said, discussions involve many comments from many sources, and it's hard to keep individuals in mind as you move from one student to another. It is not easy to reconstruct with accuracy what you heard in retrospect. To help you do this, you can tape-record discussions and review them later. When you are listening to the tapes, pay particular attention to the behaviors of students who struggle and to the *scaffolding* of ideas (how one student refers to and/or builds off others). Think also about what kinds of thoughts you hear—for example, observations, narratives/inferences, and providing evidence.

A path marker to help you chart growth over time is available on the subscription Web site: http://vtsweb.org/vts-subscriptions.

CHAPTER 5: VTS, LANGUAGE DEVELOPMENT, AND ENGLISH LANGUAGE LEARNERS

All students continue to develop their command of language throughout elementary school, though it is usually more noticeable in low-income and ELL students. VTS discussions have an impact on all of them. As teachers, you are trained to know the markers of written language development appropriate for your students, both as individuals and as a whole. You are equipped to assess what you see from students in terms of vocabulary, word use, grammar, syntax, sequence, and structure.

As you pay attention to how students speak and write during and after image discussions, you have anecdotal data to assess their capacities with language in a more holistic and authentic way than you get from traditional tests. Listening and paraphrasing allow you to appreciate students' capacities for oral expression, something that is generally sought but not explicitly taught or tested.

As you take in and reflect on students' comments, you have insight into both how they think and how they express themselves; there is a strong correspondence between the two. For example, as students make more and more detailed observations, they need more descriptive language to express their thoughts. As inferences increase in number and complexity, the students find more and more precise language to communicate. Multiple observations—especially when the student sees them as related—lead to complex sentences, as do inferences argued in evidence.

This doesn't happen overnight, and it depends on the age/stage/capacities of each student too, but it's virtually inevitable: as thinking becomes richer, language follows. Data tells us that it happens in all students. The more discussions students have—whether of art images (and the VTS organization is building its database of images for different grade levels), images of other sorts, illustrations in texts, or text itself—the more the impact is likely to be seen. To capitalize on this, most teachers who enjoy VTS lessons with art find the questions and facilitation method filtering into other lessons. Many subjects have the capacity to intrigue students who are given the chance to explore them in a constructivist, discovery mode, developing language as they explore various topics. Such beginning inquiry can be followed by more directive instruction. Importantly, it builds the use of language across disciplines.

Teachers of English as a second language are often good sources to turn to for mechanisms to monitor oral language development—that is, finding out how to attune one's listening to hear change.

CHAPTER 6: LEARNING HOW "TO VTS"

When teachers begin facilitating image discussions, the most common delights are the number of kids who participate, the way they can disagree without rancor, and how much you learn about your students. The most common challenges have to do with restraint: why can't I correct mistakes or provide information? The wisdom of restraint is pretty simple: there are times when students need to do the work on their own, and this is one of them. You're helping them learn to examine, think, listen, debate, and formulate their own ideas: these are tasks they must teach themselves, and VTS sets up a responsible, rigorous way for them to do it. You're there to help, and you do it by facilitating their discovery process, not directing it. Does this make sense?

Some teachers face logistical challenges as they start—for example, dealing with kids who dominate or ones who persistently hang back. The best way to handle these is to ask other teachers what they do; in fact, formal VTS training is virtually entirely based on teachers talking their way through the issues that come up, ranging from problems to trying to understand the learning.

As noted, VTS has two Web sites, one of which is available by subscription and has materials that directly support implementation—everything from lesson plans, images, and core readings to writing sample forms, questions to help teachers reflect after lessons, and links to blogs and networks of other teachers. Information about subscribing is available on http://vtshome.org/research. This Web site also has answers to many frequently asked questions. For example, here's part of the response to "What do I do when I hear wrong answers?":

> There will be times when you think a comment is mistaken, and in VTS, we ask you to accept such answers in the same way you respond to ones you think are on the right track. This might be challenging because it runs counter to convention. When you hear answers you think are "wrong," try to figure out what's behind them. They may mean that students see things differently from you. There may be missteps in a process that still ends up in the right place. "Wrong" answers often inform you about how a student's mind works.
>
> Here's what you have to remember: this process is not about right and wrong, but giving students the chance to explore freely. Learning to observe, think, express, and listen are what matters. Therefore, let students carry out a full process of discovery.

Some answers address questions that have to do with VTS technique. For example, "What do you mean by 'linking comments?'":

> Through linking, you help make sense of a conversation that otherwise could seem random. By pointing out ideas that agree, you make it clear that drawing the same or similar conclusions as others is often appropriate. "It seems that several people see that." Or, "Mark agrees with Kenzo that the girl's expression makes her seem contented."
>
> By linking ideas that disagree, you indicate equally clearly that it's possible for different people to respond differently to something they see. "We have a variety of opinions here." Or, "Sonia is also looking at her expression but thinks her eyes look a little sad."

By indicating how some ideas build off of others, you show the benefits of collaboration: we scaffold on the ideas and knowledge of others. "Malik agrees with Sonia but wonders if the girl might just be thinking about something." Or, "Ashley agrees that she might be sad and adds a reason: because her puppy seems to be running away, as Tyler pointed out earlier."

You can also indicate changes of mind: "Kenzo has changed his mind, convinced by Tyler's puppy story."

As you learn VTS, a good way to accomplish several things at once is to practice VTS with colleagues. From this you build your own rapport with art, get practice with facilitation, and have a forum for talking about aspects of the teaching you'd like to understand better. After conducting a practice image discussion, you can help each other by answering the following questions:

- What did you learn from and/or how did you feel about this teaching?
- Participants then answer: What made you feel good about our demonstrator's teaching?
- What can we do when [something that has gone wrong] happens?
- What are your takeaways from this experience?

You can reflect on classroom discussions by asking yourself questions like these:

- Was the image or subject a good one? Did it provoke a good discussion? What can I learn from this?
- What did I observe happening to the students? Who did less well? Who was challenged? Who excelled? What can I learn from this?
- Did I reach my objectives, fall short, or exceed them? What can I learn from this?
- How would I assess my listening? My paraphrasing? What might I improve? What might I change the next time I try this?

A second VTS site is open to the public and designed to answer questions of people generally interested in knowing more about VTS. The site contains taped discussions at many grade levels, research reports, biographies of key players, and interviews with people who have experienced VTS in their schools and lives. You can also find descriptions of professional development and the implementation process as well as contact information about those who can answer specific questions. Costs for training and materials are available upon request; the cost is modest and geared to the size of the school. The URL is http://vtshome.org/.

Professional development available from VTS takes place over three years and requires roughly twenty to twenty-four hours each year, though the specifics depend on the needs and desires of each school. While individual teachers can often find workshops in their area to help them learn VTS and may implement it on their own, much is gained by whole-school implementations because of the sequential nature of the benefits to students and because of peer interactions and mutual support among teachers.

Outline of Components of Professional Development Each Year (of a three-year span)

- *Initial training day: demonstrations and practice with coaching*
- *Teaching of ten hour-long lessons, taught once a month; ideally the last lesson is a museum visit for appropriate grade levels*
- *Three or four 2-hour debriefings spread among lessons throughout the year for reflecting on student behavior, addressing problems, practicing with coaching, and some exercises to aid paraphrasing and linking*
- *One to two coteaching visits to the classroom by the VTS trainer to provide mentoring, answer questions, deal with specific issues*

CHAPTER 7: EFFECTIVE TEACHING

Effective teaching will soon be defined by success at meeting Common Core standards, presently detailed for language and math. It won't be long before new science standards exist. The authors of Common Core have been clear that they want it left to teachers and schools to decide how to meet the new challenges, although curriculum writers will soon start taking advantage of the void. VTS is ideal for initiating the desired learning in preschool and reinforcing and extending it throughout the elementary years. Here are descriptions of behaviors in language and math sought over the course of schooling for these two subjects, taken from the Common Core explanations available online (http://www .corestandards.org):

> Students who meet the Standards readily undertake the close, attentive reading that is at the heart of understanding and enjoying complex works of literature. They habitually perform the critical reading necessary to pick carefully through the staggering amount of information available today in print and digitally . . . They reflexively demonstrate the cogent reasoning and use of evidence that is essential to both private deliberation and responsible citizenship in a democratic republic. In short, students who meet the Standards develop the skills in reading, writing, speaking, and listening that are the foundation for any creative and purposeful expression in language.
>
> One hallmark of mathematical understanding is the ability to justify, in a way appropriate to the student's mathematical maturity, why a particular mathematical statement is true or where a mathematical rule comes from . . . The student who can explain the rule understands the mathematics, and may have a better chance to succeed at a less familiar task such as expanding $(a + b + c)$ $(x + y)$. Mathematical understanding and procedural skill are equally important, and both are assessable using mathematical tasks of sufficient richness.

VTS provides a very simple and efficient means to set in motion the complicated thinking required by Common Core. Through the combination of VTS with images and applications of VTS in other lessons, you can hone essential skills in understanding, problem solving, and group process. At the same time, you give students a natural and authentic way to develop their ability to express themselves aloud and in writing. You can nurture all of this in lessons spread throughout the curriculum and support the learning over time. They can, for example, "reflexively demonstrate the cogent reasoning and use of evidence."

All of this starts with discussions of art that students enjoy; the level of engagement and joy seamlessly transfer to other lessons as the pleasure of learning in all disciplines reaches all children, from those who learn easily to those who struggle.

SUGGESTED READING

Arnheim, Rudolf. *Thoughts on Art Education*. Los Angeles: The J. Paul Getty Trust, 1989.

———. *Visual Thinking*. Berkeley and Los Angeles: University of California Press, 1969.

Bruner, Jerome Seymour. *The Process of Education*. Cambridge, MA: Harvard University Press, 1960.

———. *Toward a Theory of Instruction*. Cambridge, MA: Harvard University Press, 1966.

Common Core State Standards Initiative, www.corestandards.org.

Dewey, John. *The Child and the Curriculum*. Chicago: University of Chicago Press, 1902.

———. *Experience and Education*. New York: Kappa Delta Pi, 1938.

———. "My Pedagogic Creed." *School Journal* 54 (1897): 77–80, http://en.wikisource.org/wiki/My_Pedagogic_Creed.

Housen, Abigail. "Aesthetic Thought, Critical Thinking and Transfer." *Arts and Learning Journal* 18, no. 1 (2002): 99–132, http://vtshome.org/research/articles-other-readings.

———. "Eye of the Beholder: Research, Theory and Practice." Paper presented at the conference of Aesthetic and Art Education: A Transdisciplinary Approach, Lisbon, Portugal (sponsored by the Calouste Gulbenkian Foundation, Service of Education), September 27–29, 1999, http://vtshome.org/research/articles-other-readings.

National Commission on Excellence in Education. *A Nation at Risk: The Imperative for Educational Reform*. Washington, DC: U.S. Department of Education, 1983.

Singer, Dorothy G., and Tracy A. Revenson. *A Piaget Primer: How a Child Thinks, Revised Edition*. New York: Plume, 1996.

Toffler, Alvin. *Future Shock*. New York: Random House, 1970.

Vygotsky, L. S. *Mind in Society*. Cambridge, MA: Harvard University Press, 1978.

———. *Thought and Language*. Cambridge, MA: MIT Press, 1986.

Yenawine, Philip. "Jump Starting Visual Literacy: Thoughts on Image Selection." *Art Education* 56, no. 1 (2003): 6–12, http://vtshome.org/research/articles-other-readings.

————. "Theory into Practice: The Visual Thinking Strategies." Paper presented at the conference of Aesthetic and Art Education: A Transdisciplinary Approach, Lisbon, Portugal (sponsored by the Calouste Gulbenkian Foundation, Service of Education), September 27–29, 1999, http://vtshome.org/research/articles-other-readings.

————. "Visual Art and Student-Centered Discussions." *Theory into Practice* 37, no. 4 (1998): 314–321, http://vtshome.org/research/articles-other-readings.

NOTES

Preface

1. I had the experiences described in this book from 1995 to the present while working full-time for Visual Understanding in Education (VUE), the foundation I cofounded with Abigail Housen, Ed.D., the cocreator of VTS. VUE owns all rights, title, and interest in the trademarks "Visual Thinking Strategies" and "VTS" as well as copyrights related to VTS in various texts, syllabi, and Web sites including www.vtshome.org and www.vtsweb.org.

Chapter 1

1. Housen's research method and her findings are described in detail in various articles and reports found at http://vtshome.org/research/articles-other-readings.
2. Unknown, *Akhenaten and His Family* (with his wife Nefertiti and their three daughters under the rays of Aton), 1345 BC. Painted limestone relief from Akhetaten (Tell-el-Amarna), Egypt. Photo credit: bpk, Berlin/Aegyptisches Museum/Staatliche Museeen/Art Resource, NY. Reprinted with permission.

Chapter 2

1. David Turnley, *Father and Daughter Playing Guitar*, 1986. Color photograph. © David Turnley/CORBIS. Reprinted with permission.
2. *Cheevers Meadows and His Daughters*, 1933. Doris Ulmann Photograph Collection, PHO38_27_3257, Special Collections and University Archives, University of Oregon Libraries, Eugene, Oregon.
3. Information about VTS and how to obtain the lesson plans, images, and more is available at http://vtshome.org.
4. Ibid.

Chapter 3

1. Curva and Associates, *Artful Citizenship Project* (Miami: The Wolfsonian, Inc., 2005); Abigail C. Housen, "Aesthetic Thought, Critical Thinking and Transfer," *Arts and Learning Research Journal* 18, no. 1 (2002): 99–132. An addendum to the latter shows the concurrent reading scores as state tests were first being adopted. For summaries of these studies, see http://vtshome.org/research/research-studies.

2. These are scanned images of work sheets from three of Marion Bageant's English language learners, showing how they solved the word problems they had discussed using the VTS prompts just beforehand. Marion reports that ELL students traditionally struggle with word problems. Reprinted with permission.

3. http://www.newamerica.net/files/afghanmap.pdf.

4. You may find out more about Billy Collins's Project 180, including the poems he's recommended, at http://www.loc.gov/poetry/180/p180-home.html.

Chapter 4

1. Winslow Homer, *Snap the Whip*, 1872. Oil on canvas. Reproduced by permission of Bridgeman Art Library International.

2. http://vtshome.org/system/resources/0000/0003/Miami-FL-VTS-Study.pdf.

3. http://www.pz.gse.harvard.edu/moma.php.

4. http://vtshome.org/system/resources/0000/0069/ISGM_Summary.pdf.

5. Abigail C. Housen, "Aesthetic Thought, Critical Thinking and Transfer," *Arts and Learning Research Journal* 18, no. 1 (2001–2002): 99–132; see http://vtshome.org/programs/vts-downloads.

6. Rudolf Arnheim, *Visual Thinking* (Berkeley and Los Angeles: University of California Press, 1969), v.

7. Ibid.

8. L. S. Vygotsky, *Mind in Society* (Cambridge, MA: Harvard University Press, 1978), 86.

9. Limbourg Brothers (Herman, Pol, Jean), *November: Acorn Harvest* (detail of farmworker and hogs). Calendar miniature from the *Très Riches Heures du Duc de Berry*, 1416. © RMN-Grand Palais/Art Resource, NY. Reprinted with permission.

10. http://ati.pearson.com/authors-consultants/rick-stiggins.html.

11. http://fcat.fldoe.org/pdf/rubrcw04.pdf.

12. http://www.corestandards.org/ELA-Literacy/W/3.

Chapter 5

1. Betty Hart and Todd R. Risley, *Meaningful Differences in the Everyday Experience of Young American Children* (Baltimore: Paul H. Brookes Publishing, 1995); a synopsis is available at http://www.gsa.gov/graphics/pbs/The_Early_Catastrophe_30_Million_Word_Gap_by_Age_3.pdf.

2. L. S. Vygotsky, *Mind in Society* (Cambridge, MA: Harvard University Press, 1978), 32.

3. Ibid., 86.

4. Ibid., 84–91.

5. http://vtshome.org/system/resources/0000/0003/Miami-FL-VTS-Study.pdf.

6. Mary Cassatt, *The Child's Bath*, 1893. Oil on canvas. Robert A. Waller Fund, 1910.2, The Art Institute of Chicago. Reprinted with permission.

7. Diego Rodriguez Velazquez, *Prince Balthasar Carlos on Horseback*, 1635. Oil on canvas. Photo credit: Scala/Art Resource, NY. Reprinted with permission.

8. http://www.k12.wa.us/Writing/pubdocs/EALRwritingfinal.pdf.

9. http://msmcclure.com/?page_id=1092.

10. http://msmcclure.com/?page_id=1056.

Chapter 7

1. Alvin Toffler, *Future Shock* (New York: Random House, 1970).

2. National Commission on Excellence in Education, *A Nation at Risk: The Imperative for Educational Reform* (Washington, DC: U.S. Department of Education, 1983).

3. http://www.edtrust.org/dc/press-room/press-release/shut-out-of-the-military-more-than-one-in-five-recent-high-school-gradua.

4. http://www.gesellinstitute.org.

5. http://www.impatientoptimists.org/Topics/Early-Learning-US.

ACKNOWLEDGMENTS

THIS BOOK IS DEDICATED TO the scores of teachers who have shown us the way for the two decades VTS has been in any form of existence. To all of them, I want to say thank you (as inadequate as that short expression feels as I write it); they are heroic and deserve to be celebrated. I want to single out a few without whom this book could not have been written: Carol Henderson, Tracy McClure, Craig Madison, Elaine Chu, Marion Bageant, Brian Fizer, Kimya Jackson, Jeff Rood, Michael Baulier, Michael Gordon, Tracy Madeiros, Heather Sutherland, Debra Vigna, Rachel Zender, and Linda Sugano. I hope I have given their remarkable work a fair presentation and an appreciative audience.

No book worth reading gets to print without the support of an intelligent editor capable of the dual and conflicting responsibilities of maintaining both a broad perspective and an awareness of small details. I have been blessed with Nancy Walser at Harvard Education Press, who has managed me and this book with charm, skill, clarity, patience, and speed. She was ably joined by copyeditor Rachel Monaghan, whose keen eye caught myriad details. Many thanks to the designer, Kim Arney; the kind, tireless, and always helpful production coordinator, Sumita Mukherji; and the marketing and public relations staff responsible for getting this book out into the world: Laura Madden, Christina DeYoung, and Rose Ann Miller. I'm also more than grateful to Caroline Chauncey, who took a chance on an unsolicited draft of a book from an unknown source, helped transform a jumble of ideas into a professional book proposal, and oversaw its review by the press. I have her to thank that you have something to read.

My colleagues at VTS have been the sources of information and collaboration over many years and their contributions to this book are

185

legion: huge thanks to Karin DeSantis, Catherine Egenberger, Penelope Speier, Yoon Kang O'Higgins, Nicholas Gardner, Lisa Luri, Oren Slozberg, Elaine Chu, Gretchen Baudenbacher, Gerard Holmes, Michael Martin, Amy Chase Gulden, Liz Harvey, Robyn Muscardini, Jasie Britton, Kim Aziz, Marlene Roeder, Alexa Miller, Lee Houck, Samantha Lee, Erica Sera, and Alfredo Espinosa.

Many district administrators have paved the way for VTS in their districts: Thomas Payzant, Carol Johnson, Diane Zimmerman, Davide Celoria, Camille Bach, and Isabel Romero. Without the support of principals, VTS flounders in a school, and particular thanks go to Karen Roos, Maite Iturri, Jeff Williamson, Clinton Price, and Jean Kluver, who first introduced me to Harvard Education Press.

We've had enormous and immeasurably helpful collaboration regarding research and practice from museum colleagues over the years, too numerous to name but a few: Linda Duke, Nancy Jones, Mary Lewis, Peggy Burchenal, Kate Rawlinson, Heidi Arbogast, Dabney Hailey, Dori Jacobson, Wendy Wolf, Hope Torrents, Michelle Grohe, Paula Lynn, Willamarie Moore, Judy Murray, Judith King, and Jeanne Hoel. For the independent, corroborative research studies, thanks to Curva and Associates and the Institute for Learning Innovation.

I have long thought of Abigail Housen as my guru, and both her data, on which VTS is based, and her research methods—used to see if, when, and how it worked as well as to revise and extend it—are the reasons VTS works.

Similarly, no book gets written without the forbearance of friends, family, and colleagues. Readers of this book have now found out that it's dotted with stories of my much-adored granddaughter, Wyla, whose existence gave me the chance to rediscover the joys of early learning and many truths about the process. Her father, Tad, and her aunt, Rebecca, my original and ongoing sources of inspiration, were perfect sounding boards throughout the process of creating VTS and this book. My partner, Andrew Neave, embodies patience, support, and brilliant counsel.

My unending thanks to all of them.

ABOUT THE AUTHOR

PHILIP YENAWINE is cofounder of Visual Understanding in Education (VUE), a nonprofit educational research organization that develops and studies ways of teaching visual literacy and of using art to teach thinking and communication skills. VUE's curriculum, Visual Thinking Strategies (VTS), is in use in schools across the United States and abroad. Director of Education at the Museum of Modern Art from 1983 to 1993, Yenawine also directed education programs at the Metropolitan Museum of Art and Chicago's Museum of Contemporary Art earlier in his career. He was founding director of the Aspen Art Museum and consulting curator at the Institute for Contemporary Art in Boston. He has taught art education at the School of the Art Institute in Chicago and Massachusetts College of Art. He received the National Art Education Associations Award for Distinguished Service in 1993, was the George A. Miller Visiting Scholar at the University of Illinois in 1996, and was the first Educator-in-Residence at the Isabella Stewart Gardner Museum in 2012, among other honors. He is on the board of the Art Matters foundation. Yenawine is the author of *How to Look at Modern Art*, *Key Art Terms for Beginners*, and six children's books about art. He helps with image selection as well as acts as a moderator for the NYTimes.com Learning Network feature, "What's Going On in This Picture?"

Yenawine attended Princeton University from 1960 to 1963, and holds a BA from Governor's State University in Park Forest South, Illinois, and an MA from Goddard College in Plainfield, Vermont. He was awarded an honorary doctorate by the Kansas City Art Institute in 2003.

INDEX